TESTIMONY
to OTHERWISE

THE Witness OF
Elijah AND Elisha

WALTER BRUEGGEMANN

CHALICE™
PRESS

ST. LOUIS, MISSOURI

Cover art: "Elijah Ascends in a Chariot of Fire" by James J. Tissot, Jewish Museum, New York/SuperStock
Cover and interior design: Elizabeth Wright
Art direction: Elizabeth Wright

This book is printed on acid-free, recycled paper.

Visit Chalice Press on the World Wide Web at
www.chalicepress.com

10 9 8 7 6 5 4 3 2   03

Library of Congress Cataloging–in–Publication Data

Brueggemann, Walter.
    Testimony to otherwise : the witness of Elijah and Elisha / Walter Brueggemann.
      p.   cm.
    Includes bibliographical references.
    ISBN 0-8272-3640-9
    1. Elijah (Biblical prophet). 2. Elisha (Biblical prophet). 3. Bible. O.T. Kings—Criticism, interpretation, etc.   I. Title.
BS580.E4 B78 2001
222'.5092—dc21   2001005987

Printed in the United States of America

Contents

To the Memory
of
Eugene S. Wehrli

Preface

The recovery of biblical interpretation and preaching that is in the air now goes along with enormous momentum. While it is true that the Bible and its preaching is in every season urgent and indispensable, there are no doubt times when such interpretation and preaching are of acute importance. Ours is such a time. In the wake of the quiet 1950s when everything seemed settled and conventional, the turbulent 1960s and 1970s when the church nearly lost its nerve, and the 1980s when the ideology of greed led to immense accommodation on the part of the church, the turn of the century marks a time in the church when rethinking and fresh resolve constitute the order of the day. That new occasion especially concerns the recovery of the voice of the church in a way that is relatively unfettered and unencumbered by old habits of accommodation.

The recovery of preaching—dependent upon a fresh engagement of the authority of scripture—benefits from the work of a whole generation of homiletic thinkers and from important interpretive work in a variety of related disciplines, among them rhetorical and literary studies, sociology of knowledge, and attention to the generative power of imagination and its capacity to deconstruct and reconstruct. The transposition of these new learnings into credible practice is not an easy maneuver and is no doubt an important and continuing task that requires our best energy and discipline. I suggest that the recovery of the voice of scripture is especially urgent, given the force of electronic communication, the flattening power of technique that serves the ideology of consumerism, and the near disappearance in our society of voices of candor and hope. Thus, I understand biblical interpretation and preaching to be the sound of humanness—surely evangelical humanness—in the face of large-scale silencing, partly by default and partly by ideological design.

I consider this present book a working out in some detail of the defining importance of "testimony" that dominated my recent *Theology of the Old Testament: Testimony, Dispute, Advocacy* (Fortress Press, 1997). Since I published that book, "testimony" has increasingly emerged as a practice of "truth from below" that is profoundly democratic and that does not await any authorization from hegemonic powers, epistemological or economic. (See, for example, the important historical study of Anna Carter Florence, *Preaching As Testimony: Towards a Woman's Preaching Tradition and New Homiletical Models* [Princeton Theological Seminary Dissertation, 2000], and the programmatic lecture of Rebecca Chopp, "Theology and the Poetics of Testimony" [unpublished lecture, Emory University, 2000]). It is clear that such interpretation and preaching—that is non-foundational or, perhaps better, anti-foundational—is an offer of a new voice of transformative potential. Such interpretation and preaching, with all their spirit-led risks, constitute a deep break from old habits of reasoning and utterance. It is clear that the old "liberal habit" of a "social action agenda" has, of itself, little transformative power in the present church. It is equally clear that the old "conservative habit" of scholastic certitude makes little claim on the energies and passion of the church. No doubt the church will continue the habits of liberal advocacy and conservative certitude. But surely it is self-evident that the primary work of the utterance of the church is neither such advocacy nor such certitude, but to voice an alternative way in the world that can be ventured outside the conventions that define and posture as "given."

The argument here is in two parts. In chapters 1 and 2, I have tried to consider in a more programmatic way the need and possibility of an uttered alternative that is inescapably inchoate and "about to be" ("at hand"). In the remainder of the book, by specific textual reference I have tried to suggest that such an utterance of alternative is underway in the biblical text itself. It is the chance of the church's utterance to replicate what happens in the text itself in the present life of the church. Such textual practice seeks the formation of a missional community that is not predictable in its advocacy or in its certitude, but that allows for gifts, energies, and visions to be given by God to the church through the process of utterance. Such work requires a different disposition on the part of the church's utterers; we may celebrate in anticipation a new generation of utterers in the church who trust the text in its detail, and who know that like "the devil," the life-giving spirit is in the detail of the text and of its utterance. The materials of this book were presented as the George Leslie McKay Lectures at the Taiwan Theological Seminary. I was treated to splendid hospitality throughout the course of those lectures by many colleagues and found in my host, Dr. Yang-En Cheng, a comrade of mind and spirit. Along the way portions of these materials were presented as the James Reid Lectures at Westminster College, Cambridge, England, and as the Selwyn Lectures in the Lichfield Cathedral, England. Chapter 1 was presented as a lecture to the American Academy of Homiletics and was printed in the *Journal for Preachers* (XXIII/3, Easter 2000, pp. 3–17). Chapter 2 was prepared for and presented to the Thompson Scholars at Columbia Theological Seminary and again in a conference on "The Future of Reformed Theology" at Westminster College. Chapter 3 was prepared for and presented to the "Oasis" event sponsored by my Columbia Theological Seminary friend and colleague Ben Campbell Johnson. I am glad to acknowledge all of these earlier uses of this material, and to recall with gratitude the several occasions of good hospitality and friendship and the communities of listeners who seriously engaged my argument.

I am glad to take this occasion to recall, celebrate, and honor the memory of Eugene S. Wehrli. He was, in sequence, my first college advisor, then teacher, colleague, and seminary president, always a genuine friend, attentive neighbor, and wise supporter. He embodied all that was most faithful and most generous in my particular theological tradition of the "Evangelical Synod." Like so many others, my life is greatly different and vastly "other" in rich and deep ways because of his abiding presence among us.

Walter Brueggemann
Columbia Theological Seminary
July 12, 2000

Introduction

In my book of 1997, *Theology of the Old Testament*, I have proposed that "testimony" be taken, metaphorically understood, as the preferred and characteristic way in which ancient Israel attested to its faith in YHWH.[1] By settling on this term and the implied imagery of the courtroom, I sought to make a non-foundational or anti-foundational claim, that Israel's attestation to its God is unfettered by the restraints of conventional reason and uncurbed by any positivistic assessment of what might have "happened" in Israel's experience to which it bears witness.[2] As the courtroom drama in pursuit of truth follows the adjudication and embrace and/or rejection of testimony, so I suggest that the truth rendered in biblical faith for us as belated readers follows the adjudication and embrace and/or rejection of testimony as it is given in Israel's textual attestation. For the comfort of foundationalists who insist that such texts must be tested against universal reason, note well that I have included "adjudication" in the process of testimony, though it is not to be imagined that adjudication according to "universals" is itself innocent or disinterested.

In the following chapters it is my intention to consider quite concretely the ways in which memories of Elijah and Elisha took on a quality and authority of durable testimony in Israel. Somewhere the stories were initially told by those who claimed to be eyewitnesses to the wonders narrated here. Evidently the stories were told and retold and told again, until they achieved claim enough to qualify as "scripture." The route from initial telling to a canonical telling is, of course, completely hidden from us; the route in any case is a "chain of voices" whereby each "testifying generation" hears and trusts enough to hand on "to you as of first importance what I in turn had received…" (1 Cor. 15:3).[3] The initial confidence in these "narrative happenings" may have been among common, needy folk who "were spellbound by what they heard" (see Lk. 19:48). Subsequent retellings of these stories,

1

moreover, must have satisfied a need in a listening community that was credulous enough to entertain tales of the "impossible" when the world at hand had become unbearably wearying. We do not know why such tales that defy reason and ordinary experience are "satisfying," but they evidently met a need that caused them to be remembered, retold, and finally given canonical authority that they could not have had in any initial telling.

The way in which these stories are now situated in the books of Kings makes clear that the framers of tradition understood that these stories voice deeply contested claims. That is, the stories do not exist in a vacuum, but fully in the context of the very "royal truth" they serve to subvert.[4] Because these stories occupy so much "air time" in the books of Kings, one may imagine that the "final form of the text" intends to undermine royal renditions of reality that give frame and visible shape to the literature. That, of course, makes good sense if the text is put together with a knowing eye on the exile and the complete exhaustion of royal reality in Jerusalem that has failed or, alternatively, with dominating imperial power that sought to neutralize Israel's passion for faith.

When the prophetic narratives are understood "canonically," this may mean in "critical" terms that the texts are situated, valued, and heard precisely in the exile where the external reality of empire is beyond concrete challenge.[5] In such an environment, ancient memories of subversion may now be reheard as subversion of present imperial reality in which good prospects for Israel (as Judaism) or for the God of Israel were not evident in abundance.

The book is divided into two unequal parts. In the first two chapters I have lined out my assumptions; in the remainder of the book I have tried to show how specific texts of prophetic narratives enact the subversions I have suggested. I have sought to show that the prophetic figure, as a character in the narrative, by his very presence endlessly summons listening Israel to a radical either/or decision. That is, the prophetic figure—embedded in the prophetic narrative—asserts an imperative to choose (as in Deut. 30:15–20; Josh. 24:14–15). The community that hears such an account of reality must always again decide for the world enacted by YHWH, though a decision can of course be made to live in a pre-YHWH, non-YHWH, anti-YHWH world of despair and death. The prophetic character embedded in prophetic narrative, however, is not only an embodied imperative summons. These characters are at the same time a narrative embodiment of hope, asserting in quite concrete ways that "it could be otherwise," that they then, we are told, make it so. The narratives and their leading characters characteristically eschew any "essentialism" about social reality and exhibit the wonder of a world profoundly open to new gifts of a quite concrete kind, gifts that are not distributed according to the conventions of ordered society.

If one considers *"either/or"* as a genuine choice and *"otherwise"* as a genuine possibility, it will be evident why I believe that any foundationalist curb is alien to the narrative material, for such a curb by "universal reason" defeats and destroys the intent of the narrative. It is evident that the initial tellers of these narratives did not pause in any suspicion about the tale they told, nor did the long chain of witnesses that came finally to the canonizing process. These narratives do not speak loudly, do not argue, and do not overwhelm. They are simply there in their durable simplicity, subtly waiting to be heard yet again, making available genuine choice and genuine possibility.

1

An Imaginative "Or"

Preaching from the Old Testament

Perhaps it is unavoidable that the theme "preaching from the Old Testament" raises the sticky christological issue about finishing up Old Testament texts with reference to Jesus. The question is difficult, and I should say where I am. I believe the Old Testament does lead to the New and to the gospel of Jesus Christ. It does not, however, lead there directly, but only with immense interpretive agility. It is does not, moreover, lead there singularly and necessarily in my judgment, because it also leads to Judaism and to the synagogue with its parallel faith. I shall bracket out of my consideration the christological question implied by the title with the recognition, put in trinitarian terms, that in the Old Testament we speak of the Father of the Son.[1] As we confess the fullness of the Father manifest in the Son, so we may confess the fullness of God manifest to Israel in the Father. This is a question of endless dispute, but I owe it to you to be clear on my own conviction.

Rather than the christological question, however, I shall focus in this essay on the ecclesial question. I understand preaching to be the chance to *summon and nurture an alternative community with an alternative identity, vision, and vocation, preoccupied with praise and obedience toward the God we Christians know fully in Jesus of Nazareth.*

5

This accent on alternative community resonates with the point being made in current "Gospel and Culture" conversation, much propelled by Lesslie Newbigin's focus on election, that God in God's inscrutable wisdom has chosen a people whereby the creation will be brought to wholeness.[2] Two other beginning points are on my mind that make the community-forming work of the Old Testament peculiarly contemporary for us.

First, it is crucial to remember that the Old Testament is zealously and pervasively a Jewish book. Jews, and Israelites before them, have characteristically presented and understood themselves to be a distinct community with an alternative identity *rooted theologically and exhibited ethically*—alternative to the Egyptians, the Canaanites, the Philistines, the Assyrians, the Babylonians, the Persians, and the Hellenists; and not only alternative but always subordinate to and under threat from dominant culture.[3] Thus, I understand the intention of the Torah and prophets—and differently, I believe, also wisdom— to be insisting upon *difference*, with theological rootage and ethical exhibition. The God question is decisive, even if backgrounded, but the more urgent issues are maintenance of communal identity, consciousness, and intentionality.

Second, with the disestablishment of Western Christianity and the collapse of the social hegemony of the church, the formation of a distinctive community of praise and obedience now becomes urgent as it was not when the Western church could count on the support and collusion of dominant culture. If the church in our society is not to evaporate into an ocean of consumerism and anti-neighborly individualism, then the summons and nurture of an alternative community constitutes an emergency. Thus, with a huge *mutatis mutandis*, I propose that as the Jews lived in a perennial emergency of identity, so the church in our time and place lives in such an emergency.[4] In both cases, moreover, a primal response to the emergency and a primal antidote to assimilation and evaporation is the chance of preaching. In reflection upon the Old Testament and the ecclesial emergency, I will consider three theses.

The *Either/Or* Alternative

The summons, nurture, formation, and enhancement of an alternative community of praise and obedience depends upon the clear articulation of an "either/or," the offer of a choice and the requirement of a decision that is theologically rooted and ethically exhibited, that touches and pervades every facet of the life of the community and its members.[5] The choice is presented clearly and the response is considered urgent. I believe that this either/or belongs inevitably to an alternative community, because an alternative identity requires an endless intentionality. For without vigilance the alternative cannot be sustained. I have reflected upon Old Testament texts around this theme; my impression is that there are only rare texts that are "holding actions." Everything in Israel's text urges an alternative.

The alternative that must be embraced in order to be Israel includes the summons to Abraham and Sarah to "go," for without going there will be no land and no future, no heir and no Israel. The summons to slaves in Egypt through Moses is to "depart," for if there is no "departure" there is no promised land. Moses worries, moreover, that if Israel does not believe, it will not depart and will not be Israel (Ex. 4:1).[6] Less instantaneous but certainly pervasively, the prophets endlessly summon Israel to an alternative covenant ethic, lest the community be destroyed. And even in the wisdom traditions, the restrained advocacy of wisdom and righteousness is in the awareness that foolishness will indeed bring termination. Perhaps the most dominant statement of the either/or that belongs characteristically to the faith perspective of the Old Testament is to be found at Mount Carmel, where Elijah challenges Israel:

> How long will you go limping with two different opinions?
> If the LORD is God, follow him; but if Baal, then follow him
> (1 Kings 18:21).

We are told first,

> The people did not answer him a word (v. 21b).

But at the end they said,

> The LORD indeed is God; the LORD indeed is God (v. 39).

This text knows that Israel, in order to be the people of Yahweh, must be endlessly engaged in an intentional decision for Yahwism, a decision that fends off the powerful forces of the dominant culture.[7]

I wish now to consider in some detail two classic formulations of either/or that occur at pivot points in Israel's life. The first of these is Joshua 24, a much discussed text (which Gerhard von Rad regarded

as an ancient credo) situated as the culmination of the Hexateuch.[8]
The meeting at Shechem over which Joshua presides is set canonically
just as Israel is situated in the land. Joshua 1—12 concerns control of
the land, albeit by violence, and Joshua 13—21 concerns division of
the land among the tribes. I read this moment as Israel's arrival at
security, well-being, and affluence, as well as a rare self-congratulation.
The text is presented as a bid to non-Israelites to join up.[9] I shall
consider that a fictional staging, so that the text is in fact a bid to
Israelites in their new affluence to reembrace the faith of the Yahwistic
covenant. The text knows (as does Joshua) that there are indeed
attractive alternatives, alternatives that Israel must resist.

As von Rad saw most clearly, vv. 2–13 is a recital of Israel's core
memory.[10] It includes the ancestors of Genesis (vv. 2–4), the exodus
(vv. 5–7a), the wilderness sojourn (v. 7b), and the entry into the land
(vv. 8–13). This latter theme ends:

> I gave you a land on which you had not labored, and towns
> that you had not built, and you live in them; you eat the fruit
> of vineyards and oliveyards that you did not plant (v. 13).

It is all gift!

After this recital, the speaker (here Joshua the preacher) makes
his bid for allegiance to this particular narrative construal of reality:
"Fear and serve Yahweh in completeness and in faithfulness."
Negatively: "Put away the other gods." Positively: "Serve Yahweh."
Choose: If Yahweh…if not, then option (a) is the gods of the Euphrates
valley; option (b) is the Amorite gods in the land. Choose! Then says
the preacher, "those in my household will serve Yahweh," and will
put our lives down in the Yahweh narrative just recited. But if you
refuse this narrative, then live with the consequences and put your
life down somewhere else. No doubt the entire Hexateuch has been
pointed toward this moment. The Pentateuch consists in the live
narrative of Yahweh that generates a world of gift, liberation, and
demand, about which decisions must be made.[11]

Then follows in vv. 16–24 a dialogue about "church growth."
The exchange of Joshua and the community is a negotiation about
the either/or.

> People (vv. 16–18): Far be it from us to serve other gods…we
> will serve Yahweh. [12]

Joshua (vv. 19–20): You cannot do it. It is too hard and Yahweh is more ferocious than you imagine. [No growth seduction here.]

People (v. 21): No, we are committed. We will serve Yahweh.

Joshua (v. 22a): You are witnesses…you are on notice.

People (v. 22b): Yes we are.

Joshua (v. 23) with an imperative:

> Negative: Put away foreign gods.[13]
> Positive: Extend your hearts to Yahweh.
> Conclusion (v. 25): Joshua made a covenant with Torah demands.

This particular crisis of *either/or* is negotiated and Israel comes to be, yet again, an intentional alternative community, alternative to the gods of the land.

The second case of *either/or* that I cite is in Second Isaiah. This wondrous text is situated in the exile. In other words, the context is exactly the opposite of Joshua 24. There it was excessive security in the land. Here it is complete displacement from the religious, cultural supports of Jerusalem, set down in an ocean of Babylonian seductions and intimidations, with effective Babylonian economics and seemingly effective Babylonian gods. No doubt many deported Jews found it easier to be a Babylonian Jew, and for some that status was only a transition to becoming Babylonian. The lean choice of remaining Jews embedded in Yahweh depended upon having the *either/or* made plain, for without the *either/or*, cultural accommodation and assimilation go unchecked.

It is precisely the work of Second Isaiah to state the alternative, so that Jews tempted by Babylon have a real choice available to them. The text of Second Isaiah is well known to us; unfortunately Handel did it so that the *either/or* is not at all visible. The recurring accent of Second Isaiah is that it is now the emergency moment when Jews may and must depart Babylon. In our historical criticism, we have focused much on Cyrus and the overturn of Babylon by the Persians, so that the emancipation of the Jews is a geopolitical event. No doubt there is something in that. But I suggest not so much, because the primal departure from Babylon is not geographical, but imaginative, liturgical, and emotional: imagine Jewishness, imagine distinctiveness that has not succumbed to the pressures and seductions of the empire. From this familiar poetry of departure and distinctiveness, I will mention four characteristic elements.

1. The initial announcement, "comfort, comfort," is an assertion to Jews displaced by Yahweh's anger that caring embrace by Yahweh is now the order of the day:

> For a brief moment I abandoned you, but with great compassion I will gather you (54:7).

The Jews in exile are addressed as the forgiven, as the welcomed, as the cherished. They had pondered, for two generations, rejection by Yahweh. But to be forgiven, welcomed, and cherished invites the reembrace of Jewishness. The poet, moreover, draws out the scenario of wondrous, jubilant, victorious procession back to Jerusalem, back to Jewishness, back to alternative identity (40:3–8). It is in this reassertion and reenactment of Jewishness that the glory of Yahweh is revealed before all flesh. These Jews in this uncommon identity, moreover, are surrounded by the God who leads like a triumphant general and the God who does the rearguard pick up in order to salvage the dropouts:

> See, the Lord GOD comes with might,
> and his arm rules for him...
> He will feed his flock like a shepherd;
> he will gather the lambs in his arms,
> and carry them in his bosom,
> and gently lead the mother sheep. (40:10–11)

The purpose of the poetic opener is to permit the community to reexperience the embracive quality of Jewishness welcomed in its peculiarity.

2. In order to create imaginative space for Jewishness, the poet employs two kinds of rhetorical strategies.[14] First, it is important to debunk the vaunted powers of Babylon. This is done by teasing and mocking the gods of the empire. In 46:1–2, the gods are mocked as dumb statues that must be carried around on the backs of animals, like so many meaningless floats in a May Day parade. The ridicule is like the old humor at the chiefs of the former Soviet Union or the mocking of "whitey" that African Americans have had do for their own health and sanity. Or the poet holds a mock trial in order to show how weak

and ineffectual are the imperial gods who are passive, silent, and dormant—failures who can do neither good nor evil (41:21–29). The intention of such speech is to dress down the powers of domination, to exhibit courage in the face of power, to show that the choice of Babylon that looks so impressive is in the end sheer foolishness.

3. This debunking is matched by the vigorous reassertion of Yahweh as the most reliable player in the struggle for the future. In the salvation oracles, this poet has Yahweh repeatedly say to terrified Jews, "Fear not." "Fear not, I am with you." "Fear not, I will help you." "Fear not," be a Jew. The poet knows that the empire traffics in fear and intimidation with its uniforms, its parades, its limousines, its press conferences, its agents with dark glasses, and its intrusions in the night. All are nothing, because Yahweh is the great Equalizer who creates safe space and overrides the threat of dominant claims.

4. Finally, looking back on the highway of chapter 40 and the safe return with "fear not" that the dumb Babylonian gods cannot stop— nothing can stop resolved Jewishness—the poem announces the departure:

> Depart, depart, go out from there (52:11)!

They could remember the ancient "departure" from Egypt, remember every passover by means of unleavened bread. The lack of leavening recalled that they left in a hurry, with no time for the yeast to rise. This is a like emergency and a like departure. Except,

> For you shall not go out in haste,
>   and you shall not go in flight;
> for the LORD will go before you,
>   and the God of Israel will be your rear guard (52:12).

No rush. Leave at your convenience. First-class passengers may board at their leisure for the journey back to full, alternative Jewishness:

> For you shall go out in joy,
>   and be led back in peace (55:12).

They might not depart the emotional grip of Babylon on the day they first hear the poem; but the poetry lingers. Alternative identity, even in places of threat and seduction, is embraced as the invitation does its proper work.

The *Either/Or* of Distinctive Identity

The either/or of distinctive identity for praise and obedience is not self-evident in the nature of things, but depends completely and exclusively upon the courageous utterance of witnesses who voice choices and invite decisions where none were self-evident. My accent on the urgency of preaching the either/or is grounded in my conviction that Israel lives by a certain kind of utterance, without which Israel has no chance to live. It is for this reason that I have insisted in my recent book on Old Testament theology that Old Testament claims for God finally do not appeal to historical facticity or to ontology, but rely upon the utterance of witnesses to offer what is not self-evident or otherwise available.[15] This is indeed "theology of the word," by which I mean simply and leanly and crucially utterance.

I take as my primary case Second Isaiah, admittedly an easy case; but I would extrapolate from Second Isaiah to claim the entire Old Testament is utterance that expresses *either/or* that is not self-evident.[16] The massive hegemony of Babylon—political, economic, theological—had, so far as we know, well-nigh driven Jewishness from the horizon; and with the elimination of Jewishness it had vetoed Yahweh from the theological conversation. It is the intention of every hegemony to eliminate separatist construals of reality that are endlessly inconvenient and problematic, and certainly a separatism as dangerous as Jewishness that endlessly subverts. The tale of Daniel, perhaps later but clearly reflective of the Babylonian crisis, tells the tale of how Nebuchadnezzar is enraged that Jews should refuse imperial allegiance and hold to their odd alternative claim (Dan. 3:13–15).

This power of hegemony, moreover, matched the exiles' own sense of things, for they also had concluded that Yahweh was not engaged or worth trusting:

> Why do you say, O Jacob,
>   and speak, O Israel,
> "My way is hidden from the LORD,
>   and my right is disregarded by my God"? (40:27).

> But Zion said, "The LORD has forsaken me,
>   my Lord has forgotten me" (49:14).

> Is my hand shortened, that it cannot redeem?
>   Or have I no power to deliver? (50:2).

It is in such an environment of hegemony-cum-despair that the utterance of *either/or* takes place. It is the utterance of *either/or* that shapes the perceptual field of Israel anew, to become aware of resources not recognized, of dangers not acknowledged, and of choices that had not seemed available. I shall consider this new, subversive voice of *either/or* in two waves. First, Second Isaiah himself, perhaps someone arisen out of a continuing seminar on the text of First Isaiah, is now moved to generate and extrapolate new text. "Moved," I say, because some think it was by an out-of-the-ordinary confrontation in "the divine council," so that when the voices say, "Cry…what shall I cry…get you up on a high mountain, herald of good tidings," the one moved by divine imperative is none other than Second Isaiah, who moves out from this theological experience to reshape the lived emergency of Israel.

It is this poet who gives to the rhetoric of the synagogue and church the term "gospel."[17] Indeed, I suggest provisionally that gospel is the offer of an *either/or* where none seemed available. So in 40:9:

> Get you up to a high mountain,
>   O Zion, herald of *gospel tidings*,
> lift up your voice with strength,
>   O Jerusalem, herald of *gospel tidings*,
> lift it up, do not fear. (author trans.)

The gospeler is twice named. The gospeler, moreover, is given the utterance to be sounded: "Behold, your God," or in NRSV, "Here is your God." It is the exhibit of Yahweh as God of the exiles in a context where Babylon had banished the God of the exiles so that there were only Babylonian gods available. The news is that Yahweh is back in play, creating choices. Yahweh is back in play on the lips of the one moved to new utterance.

That text in 40:9 is matched in 52:7 in a better-known utterance:

> How beautiful upon the mountains
>   are the feet of the *gospel messenger*
>   who announces peace,
> who brings *gospel news*,
>   who announces salvation,
>   who says to Zion, "Your God reigns." (author trans.)

Again the term gospel is twice used, and again the lines are given: "Your God reigns," or better, "Your God has just become king." The line is a quote from the Psalms (see 96:10), but the utterance here is an assertion that in the contest for domination, the gods of the empire have been defeated and the God of Israel is now the dominant force in creation. The poet creates an environment for choice, for decision, for homecoming, for new, faithful action, none of which is available or choosable without this utterance.

It is, however, the second layer of utterance in this poetry that interests me, namely that the Israelites are summoned by the poet to be witnesses, to give testimony about the Yahwistic alternative about which they did not know and which the Babylonians certainly could never tolerate. In 43:8–13, the poet offers a contest among the gods. Negatively, he invites the Babylonians to give evidence for their gods: "Let them bring forth their witnesses" (v. 9, author trans.). Then in v. 10: "You are my witnesses," you exiles. You are the ones who are to speak my name, confess my authority, obey my will, accept my emancipation, tell my miracles. The exiles who themselves had thought there was no *or* to the Babylonian *either* are now called to testify to this Yahwistic *or*. There are two quite remarkable features to this poem authorizing Israel's testimonial utterance about an alternative that the empire cannot tolerate.

First, the summons and authorization to testify is interwoven with *the substance of testimony* that is to be given:

> Before me no god was formed,
> > nor shall there be any after me.
> I, I am the LORD,
> > and besides me there is no savior…
> I am God, and also henceforth I am He;
> > there is no one who can
> > > deliver from my hand;
> I work and who can hinder it? (vv. 10b–11, 13)

What is to be said is that Yahweh is the alpha and the omega, the first and the last, the creator, the one who is utterly irresistible. Note well that this extravagant claim allows no room for any Babylonian gods. In the statement of the *either/or*, the Babylonian *either* is dismissed as an irrelevant fantasy. There is only the Yahwistic *or* as an option.

Now, we might suspect that this is a frontal assault to convince the Babylonians. Perhaps so. But the second feature I observe in v. 10 is this:

> You are my witnesses, says the LORD,
>   and my servant whom I have chosen,
> so that you may know and believe me
>   and understand that I am he.

Notice: You are my witnesses…in order that…*you may know, believe, understand!*

The giving of testimony is to claim the ones who testify. Israel is to enunciate the Yahwistic option so that they themselves should trust and embrace that option. This is surely the most direct claim I know concerning Paul's assertion that faith comes from what is heard (Rom. 10:17); where there is not speaking and hearing of an alternative world, there is no faith, no courage, no freedom to choose differently, no community of faith apart from and even against the empire.

The other remarkable text is 44:8, followed by the negative of 44:9. It is clear that vv. 8 and 9 belong to quite different literary units; they are joined together perhaps to make the point about utterance. Verse 8 asserts yet again, "You are my witnesses." The last two lines of the verse, just as we have seen in chapter 43, outline the utterance that is to be uttered:

> Is there any god besides me?
>   There is no other rock; I know not one.

The testimony is that there is not only a choice outside Babylon. It is the only real choice. The new feature here, after chapter 43, is the first line of the verse to the witnesses now being recruited:

> Do not fear, or be afraid.

One can imagine a whistle-blower against a great corporation, who must say in court what the company cannot tolerate, being briefed by a lawyer: "Do not be afraid." Or a woman in a rape trial, who must give evidence but is terrified both of the shame and of the continuing threat of the rapist, being counseled: "Do not fear." The lawyer must encourage and reassure. Every witness, every serious preacher, every exile who speaks against hegemony knows the fear.

And Yahweh says, State the *or*, because it is true. Many witnesses discover, of course, that Yahweh in the end has no "witness protection program," but the witness is often compelled to give evidence nonetheless.

The negative of v. 9 is surprising. Verses 9–20 constitute an odd unit that mocks the makers of idols, the Babylonians who manufacture powerless gods. Verse 9 speaks of idols and then of witnesses, that is, the Babylonian gods and the Babylonians who champion them or Jews who trust those imperial gods too much. The idols are, with the NRSV, "nothing." The term looks like a simple rejection. But the Hebrew word is *tôhû* = chaos. The Babylonian gods are embodiments of chaos, forces of disorder. This is a remarkable claim, for the empire had claimed to be a great sponsor of order and well-being. But here it is clear: the spiritual force of the empire is against *shalom*, against peace and order and well-being. The *tôhû* of Babylon, of course, is to be contrasted with the power of the true creator God, Yahweh. Finally it is asserted that the witnesses who champion the gods of *tôhû* neither see nor know. They are so narcotized and mesmerized by the empire that they cannot see what is going on. The contrast is total, no overlap between these two god offers. The exiles can choose either *the gods of the empire* who will never deliver the well-being they claim to sponsor, or *the God of the news* who stands against all things fearful. The battle for Jewishness in exile is acute, a battle that, so it seems to me, is now replicated in the battle for baptism in an ocean of military consumerism that generates endless layers of chaos in the name of prosperity.

To be sure, Second Isaiah is an easy case for *either/or* through utterance. But I would argue that the theme is pervasive in the text of this people always struggling for its identity. I mention two kinds of evidence. First, perhaps you noticed in my longish comment on Joshua 24 that Joshua and his counterparts finally get serious precisely about testimony. He says to them:

> You are witnesses against yourselves that you have chosen the
> LORD, to serve him (v. 22).

The answer: "Witnesses." The Hebrew is terse, without a nominative pronoun. My point is a simple one: everything depends upon utterance. The dramatic occasions of teaching and preaching where the *either/or* is spelled out and sometimes embraced are serious occasions. Serious not simply because of formal oath or because we claim to be speaking true. Serious elementally because *what we say* and *how we say* is the world we receive. Israel's serious oath is to choose the *or* of Yahweh and now to hold to it (see also v. 27).

It would be nice if the *either/or* were simply out there in the landscape. Israel, however, knows better. It is here, in speech. If it is not uttered, it is not available. If it is not uttered, it is not. This point, that human possibility resides in utterance, it seems to me, is crucial not only for preaching, but more generally in a technological society.[18] Our technological mindset wants to thin, reduce, and eventually silence serious speech. The urgency of preaching and all the utterance of the church and the synagogue, I suggest, is that we know intuitively that where there is not face-to-face truth-telling, we are by that much diminished in the human enterprise. And Joshua insists, Israel must stand by its utterance.[19]

The *Or* of Open Imagination

While the *either/or* may be uttered frontally, *the or of Yahweh is characteristically spoken in figure*, because it is a possibility "at hand" but not yet in hand.[20] The *either/or* of Yahwism is directly utterable, and I have cited cases of such direct utterance. Characteristically, however, it is not done tersely and confrontationally, because such utterance is too lean, gives the listeners few resources for the tricky negotiation between options, and because the *either/or* has no one shape or form, always different with different folk in different circumstances. Moreover, while the *either* of hegemony is visible and can be described in some detail, the *or* of Yahweh does not admit of flat description because it is not yet visible, not yet in hand, always about to be, always under construal, always just beyond us. Indeed, if the *or* of Yahweh could be fully and exhaustively described, the prospect is that it would become, almost immediately, some new hegemonic *either*, as is often the case if creeds are heard too flatly, if liturgies are held too closely, if ethics is turned to legalism, if piety becomes self-confidence and pride. It is this open act of imagination in the service of a demanding, healing *or* that is the primary hard work of the preacher and the wonder of good preaching that is communicated in modes outside hegemonic certitude.

I will return to my two major cases and then in conclusion note three other places where one can see some playfulness at work in utterance.

I have characterized Joshua 24 as a primary model of *either/or* in which testimonial utterance is evident. That utterance of *either/or* in solemn assembly by Joshua culminates in v. 25: "So Joshua made a covenant with the people that day, and made statutes and ordinances for them at Shechem." The verse tells us almost nothing of what constitutes the new obedience to which Israel is pledged after this hard-won decision to embrace Yahweh's *or*. I suggest that because Joshua 24 is about the immediate settlement in the land, the Torah of Deuteronomy is the figurative articulation that fleshes out the *either/or* announced in Joshua 24. For the sake of that connection, I make two critical observations. First, it is generally agreed that Deuteronomy constitutes the norm for the "history" offered in Joshua, Judges, Samuel, and Kings, the "Deuteronomic" account of Israel's life in the land.[21] Thus, the linkage between Deuteronomy and Joshua 24 is entirely plausible, that Joshua 24:25 alludes to that Torah. Second, because Deuteronomy is "Deuteronomic," we are free to say that its framing is fictive, that the staging of the speech of Moses at the Jordan is an invitation for Israel that has embraced the Yahwistic *or* against the Canaanite *either* to conjure what the land of promise would be like were it alternatively organized and practiced in covenant. This delivers us from needing to insist that Israel enacted all these laws, but it also permits us to see the "laws" as acts of imagination in which each successive generation of *or* is to explore how to take this text into its own concrete life and practice.

I shall comment on three texts from Deuteronomy. The ones I have selected are perhaps easy cases, but the point will be more generally clear. Joshua counts on the clear *either/or* worked in detail by Moses:

1. *Either* let the economy work unfettered so that the rich become richer, *or* read Deuteronomy 15:1–18 concerning the "Year of Release."[22] Moses, in this text, anticipates and imagines that the economy of the land of Canaan does not need to be organized in exploitative "Canaanite" ways, but could be reorganized in neighborly Israelite ways. He offers a scenario for a society in which poor people must work off their debts (no doubt at high interest rates), but a neighborly ethic proposes that at the end of six years, the debt is canceled and the poor person is invited back into the economy.

> Moses said, "There will always be poor people, so you must take this seriously and keep doing it all the time" (v. 11);

Moses said, "If you do it effectively, you can eliminate such demeaning poverty and the poor will cease out of the land" (v. 4);

Moses said, "Do not entertain mean thoughts and begin to count toward the seventh year and act in hostility" (v. 9);

Moses said, "Do not only cancel the debt but give the poor a generous stake so that they can reenter the economy viably, not from the bottom up" (vv. 7–10);

Moses said, "If this seems outrageous to you, remember that you were bond-servants in Egypt and you were released by the generous power of Yahweh your redeemer who brought you out" (v. 15, author paraphrases).

This is the most radical *or* in the Bible, insisting that the economy must be embedded in a neighborly human fabric. Almost all of us choose the *either*, imagining that Joshua's *or* is not relevant to an urban, post-industrial economy. But there it sits, always a summons, always a reminder, always an invitation. And Joshua had already said, "I tried to talk you out of this *or;* I told you it was too difficult for you.

2. *Either* let legitimate authority run loose in self-serving acquisitiveness, *or* read Deuteronomy 17:14–20 concerning monarchy. It is the only law of Moses on kingship. Moses agrees only reluctantly to let Israel have a king; he thought kingship was a bad idea and all available models of centralized power were bad. Then he says, but if you must, your king, your Israelite, covenantal, neighborly king shall be different. This king, embedded in covenant, must not accumulate silver or gold or horses or chariots or wives. Moses knows the three great seductions are money, power, and sex, all of which make community impossible if they are accumulated. And so he offers an *or*. The king, when in office, shall sit all day, every day, reading Torah, meditating day and night on what Yahweh intends, on how covenantal community can curb raw power.

Israel, like every government since, found it difficult to choose this *or*. The kings of Israel characteristically took the *either* of raw power, as has every kind of authority...priests, parents, teachers, deans, bishops, corporate executives, and on and on. In Israel, the primal example of the power of greed is Solomon—gold, gold, gold, 300 wives, 700 concubines; and later it was said, "Do not be anxious, even Solomon in all his vast royal apparatus was not as well off as a bird."[23] The *or* is about power and governance and greed; in the end, however, it is about anxiety, getting more, keeping more while the land is lost in dread, terror, and devouring.[24]

3. *Either* it is every man [*sic*] for himself at the expense of all the others, *or* read Deuteronomy 24:19–22. It is about the triangle of *landowner, land,* and *landless,* and how they will live together. The *either* of Canaanite agriculture is just a "labor pool" of those nameless ones without any leverage or fringe benefits, who work but fall farther and farther behind, until they drop into welfare and then out of welfare into drugs, alcohol, sometimes a threat to us, often an inconvenience, always a nuisance and embarrassment. *Or,* says Moses, in your economic operations, leave enough for *the alien, the widow, the orphan.* Leave the sheaves of wheat when you are "bringing in the sheaves," for *the alien, the widow, the orphan.* When you beat your olive trees, leave enough for *the alien, the widow, the orphan.* When you gather grapes, leave some for *the alien, the widow, the orphan.* The triad is like a mantra for this covenantal *or.* Because Moses knows that the powerful are in common destiny with the powerless. The haves are linked to the future of the have-nots. Moses had already said, "Same law for citizens and undocumented workers" (Lev. 19:34). Moses knew that in a patriarchal society women without husbands and children without fathers are lost to the community, as bad off as outsiders.

The *or* requires a break with the orthodoxy of individualism. It requires a rejection of the notion of the undeserving poor. It requires a negation of all the pet ideologies whereby unburdened freedom is the capacity to disregard neighbor. And it is all there in the deep command of Yahweh…not socialism, not liberalism, not ideology, just an alternative life.[25]

Our Christian strategy for disposing of the Mosaic law is to dismiss it as legalism, certain we are justified by grace alone. Except that this obedience belongs to the center of an alternative community. The *or* is demanding but not obvious. The mantra of this community is endlessly "Love God, then love neighbor, neighbor, neighbor."

4. I have characterized Isaiah 40—55 as a primary model of *either/or* in which testimonial utterance gives the possibility of life to this special community that is almost succumbing to Babylon. It was to this little

community without confidence and almost without conviction that the poet declared on Yahweh's behalf:

> Because you are precious in my sight,
>   and honored, and I love you,
> I give people in return for you,
>   nations in exchange for your life (Isa. 43:4).

Second Isaiah, however, only provides the trigger for liturgical, emotional, imaginative, perhaps geographical, homecoming. When the Jews did come back to Jerusalem in 537 or 520 or 444, Second Isaiah gave little guidance. But then, Second Isaiah never comes without Third Isaiah. I propose that Third Isaiah, Isaiah 56—66, is the figurative articulation that fleshes out the *either/or* of Second Isaiah.[26] There is now a great deal of ferment about the book of Isaiah. It is increasingly likely, in scholarly judgment, that the old, deep separation of Second and Third Isaiah cannot be sustained. And therefore in its canonical shaping, one may see Isaiah 56—66 as an attempt to enact the glorious vision of Second Isaiah; but enactments must always come to detail.

1. *Either* be a community of like-minded people who are convinced of their own purity, virtue, orthodoxy, and legitimacy, excluding all others, *or* read Isaiah 56:3–8. There were all around the edges of restored Judaism inconvenient people who had no claim to purity, virtue, orthodoxy, or legitimacy. There were latecomers, not good Jews with pedigrees, who had joined in, drawn to the faith, perhaps Samaritans or whatever, but surely not "qualified." Worse than that, there were people with marked, scarred, compromised genitals, people who had sold out to Babylon in order to become willing eunuchs with access to power. Of these Moses long ago in Deuteronomy 23:1 had declared that people with irregular sexual dispositions were excluded. It is there in the Torah. All around were hovering people not like us, claiming and pushing and yearning and even believing…What to do?

Says the *or* of Third Isaiah: Have a generous spirit and a minimum but clear bar of admission. Tilt toward inclusiveness with only two requirements. That they keep covenant, that is submit to the neighborly intention of Yahweh, and that they keep sabbath, rest from the madness of production and consumption as a sign of confidence in Yahweh's governance. That's all! It is the *or* of inclusiveness, no other pedigree, no sexual transposition, no other purification, an *or* that says the community is not made in the image of our strong points. The community teems with people who score irregularly on every Myers-Briggs notion of how we are and how we ought to be.[27]

2. *Either* become a punctilious community of religious discipline, engaging in religious scruple with amazing callousness about the real world of human transaction, *or* read Isaiah 58:1–9 and consider an alternative religious discipline of fasting that is not for show or piety or self-congratulations. Practice fast that commits to the neighbor, specifically the neighbor in need, the neighbor boxed in injustice and oppression. Break the vicious cycles of haves and have-nots that produce hungry people and homeless poor and naked people, the most elemental signs and gestures of exposure, vulnerability, and degradation, produced by a system that does not notice.

Conventional religious disciplines that feel like virtue are disconnected. The practitioners of such self-congratulation, all the while, exploit and oppress and quarrel, uncaring, unthinking, unnoticing. And now the *or* of engagement that moves to solidarity with the exposed and the vulnerable. The NRSV says "they are your kin," but the Hebrew says "flesh," your own flesh of flesh and bone of bone, self of self. That is who they are.

When the lines of separation between haves and have-nots are broken by true fast, then, says Third Isaiah, then, only then, not until then:

> *Then* your light shall break forth like the dawn,
>   and your healing shall spring up quickly;
> your vindicator shall go before you,
>   the glory of the LORD shall be your rear guard.
> *Then* you shall call, and the LORD will answer;
>   you shall cry for help,
>   and he will say, Here I am. (vv. 8–9)

Then, then, then, then…it is the *or* of communion. There is, however, no communion with Yahweh until there is community with neighbor.[28]

3. *Either* cling to the old status quo of social arrangements and miss God's newness, *or* read Isaiah 65:17–25. The *or* of poetic imagination

asserts that the old heaven and the old earth and the old Jerusalem, that the old holy city and every old holy city and every old city and every old power arrangement is on the way out and is being displaced. The *or* of world renewal and urban renewal is a fantasy. The community of *or* engages in a strong act of vision: "We have a dream." It is a dream of joy and well-being, a dream in which there are no more cries of distress, no more infant mortality, no more social dislocation when people build houses and lose them to taxation, war, ethnic cleansing, or Olympic committees, where people do not plant gardens and have to move before harvest time. In the world coming, no more anguish in childbirth. And to top it all, reconciliation of creation, lions and lambs, immediate communion with and attentiveness from Yahweh, who answers before we call.

The poet offers a breathtaking *or*. He has been radical in chapter 56 on eunuchs and in 58 on poor people. But now in chapter 65 he no longer has time for the conventions of reality as he is off on a poetic, evangelical fantasy of what might be and what will be and what is at hand, but not in hand. He imagines, counter to the lovers of the old city who have not yet noticed (felt, but not noticed) the brutal dysfunction of the old city. All will be changed. The poet can scarcely see its shape, but he has no doubt that its coming shape is a healing of all old abrasions and despairs. This *or* will never happen among us while we are bound to what was. Thus, the poem is more like a parable then a blueprint, but a parable to be ingested by reforming Judaism, a parable,

about a banquet,

about a rich man and a barn,

about a man with two sons,

about a neighborly foreigner who paid the bills,

about a nagging widow,

about day laborers who get full pay.[29]

None of that is visible yet. Indeed, none of that is possible...yet. Except for those who depart from present circumstance toward the newness God will give.

Daunting as the *or* of Joshua and Second Isaiah are, the large *either/or* comes down to cases that tease and invite and haunt and wait. While I have picked two more or less obvious cases, I believe it is not different elsewhere. So finally three other suggestions that I will not pursue in detail:

4. The ancestral narratives in Genesis 12—36 (37—50) are about a son and an heir, an entry to the future, always given nearly too late. This dysfunctional family with triangles of tension and quarrels over the estate is always at the brink of despair, always wondering if there is a land or a future, or if this is the last generation.

The narratives are a tease out of despair into Yahweh's possibility. Yahweh poses the deep question to Abraham and Sarah: "Is anything impossible for Yahweh?" (Gen. 18:14). The community ponders the question. Where the answer is "Yes, some things are impossible," we get a world of fear, anxiety, greed, selfishness, and impossibility. The *or* of faith, as father Abraham came to know, is that nothing is impossible for God, and therefore despair is out of order (Lk. 1:27; 18:27).

5. The narrative of David and his family in Second Samuel 9—20, commonly called "The Succession Narrative," is a sordid account of our royal family, not different from any power family, something like Peyton Place. The plot is triggered by the Uriah incident and then a series of acts of incest, murder, usurpation of power, and concubines, culminating in the triumph of Solomon, a violent coup. It is difficult to see an *or* in this narrative, unless while you hear the story you also hear the choir chanting the messianic wonders of the Psalter. I have come to think, given my larger argument, that the *either* of these stories is violence and the *or* of alternative is the self-sacrifice of justice. The temptation to violence is pervasive among us, and these narratives have such power for us because they are so close to us. The narrator, all through this sordid account, dares the view that in, with, and under the violence there is another purpose at work.

6. The Proverbs are not exactly rich homiletical material for most of us. They are, however, not mere pragmatism or prudence. They understand that foolishness is, as von Rad nicely says, practical atheism, the attempt to live in the world on one's own.[30] Such foolishness is endlessly destructive and suicidal. The wisdom teachers tease out the *or* of wisdom—in myriad cases about wealth and sex and food and work and speech and anger and honor and shame and doubt and war and knowledge. The *or* is partly shrewdness, partly discernment, partly

faith, partly trust, partly vulnerability. The wisdom teachers keep at it, until the tombstone of humanity does not have to say with Easter pathos:

> Oh, how foolish you are, and how slow of heart to believe all that the prophets have declared (Lk. 24:25).

Impossible Possibility

I am taking an ecclesial agenda because for too long, so it seems to me, christological certitude in the church has much of the time been permitted to silence, trump, and give closure to the Old Testament. I have wanted to suggest that faithful Christian exposition could do otherwise. I regard the preacher's engagement with the Old Testament as urgent:

> because the *or* of faith, so deeply pondered by ancient Israel, is needed in the face of our dominant *either;*

> because in a technological society, it is mostly left to the preacher, who labors at it locally, to voice the human options in a crisis of flatness;

> because preachers, more than any other, have endless opportunity for the tease of detail whereby the *or* of the gospel may be received and embraced.

The *or* is an impossible possibility. Both Israel and the church have always known that. That is what makes preaching both foolish and urgent.

2

The Faithfulness of "Otherwise"

With the collapse of Christendom the church is now in a quite changed interpretive context where new ways of knowing and speaking and living are both required and permitted. Specifically, *imagination* is increasingly recognized and valued as a way in which we are led and transformed by God's category-shattering, world-forming spirit. "Imagination" may be understood as the God-given, emancipated capacity to picture (or image) reality—God, world, self—in alternative ways outside conventional, commonly accepted givens.[1] Imagination is attentiveness to what is "otherwise," other than our taken-for-granted world.[2]

The Refusal of Otherwise

Because of the endless pressure and the insatiable need to control, it is our human wont to establish a fixed, visible, settled "given" that is beyond criticism or reexamination, a "given" that variously partakes of intellectual, socioeconomic, political, and believing components.[3] A primary stratagem for securing and defending such givenness is the refusal of any "otherwise," any alternative, along with the rejection of the procedures whereby "otherwise" might be made visible and/or credible.

In broad sweep one can identify the following efforts at such visible settled givenness that intends to fend off the threat of alternative:

1. The medieval system of the church, which came to be expressed in scholastic doctrinal formulation and in sacramental administrative exclusiveness, offered a secure and certain habitat for the faithful. As it settled and developed interpretive hedges, this system became less and less open to "otherwise," and found convincing warrants and means to preclude imaginative acts of interpretation outside the givens.

2. That medieval system of teaching and sacrament, over a long and complicated time, came to be displaced in public perception by the "Age of Reason," variously termed "modernity" or "Enlightenment," which was, among other things, a response to the shambles of the religious wars. Scientific method, coupled with autonomous reason, was seen to be safer and more reliable than the old faith, which appeared to be grounded in superstition and blind tradition and was productive of bloody hostility.[4]

The logic of modernity—of which we are all children—is now belatedly seen to be exceedingly thin and one-dimensional, giving credence to the thought and judgment of "clear thinkers" who fenced out all emotion, who claimed they were objective and free of every vested interest, and who therefore became the voices of "the given."[5] This way of thinking depended upon a logic that allowed no interpretive maneuverability or upon clear, unambiguous experience that made things plain. This judgment was explicitly aimed, in the seventeenth century, at the church's claims of mystery and holiness. In terms of epistemology, it resisted any practice of imagination, of alternative picturing, because rationality demanded dealing with "the given."[6]

There are many pointers to the spent character of that certitude. I will refer to only one. United States foreign policy, rooted in the imperial dreams of Theodore Roosevelt and Elihu Root culminated in Franklin Roosevelt and Henry Stimson and his several proteges who managed the American Dream into and through the Cold War. In a remarkable book, Walter Isaacson and Thomas Evan have traced the monopoly of influence on U.S. foreign policy of six men in Washington—Dean Acheson, Charles Bohlen, Averell Harriman, George F. Kennan, Robert Lovett, and John J. McCloy.[7] What interests me is that they are termed "the Wise Men," the clearest thinkers who knew best and who framed and conducted U.S. foreign policy with cold, clear rationality, utter reasonableness. The book ends, inevitably, with the sorry scene of the Lyndon Johnson White House, in which this little cadre of "The Best and the Brightest" came repeatedly to meetings in a growing stupor, finally facing the fact that it was their "wisdom" that led to the sorriness of Vietnam, the awareness that their empty rationality—that had become uncritical ideology—did not understand and could not understand the odd fabric of humanness that had defeated their technology.

A footnote may be added. In his pathos-filled retrospective, Robert McNamara, a principal architect of the Vietnam effort, reflects in print on the self-deception of the entire enterprise.[8] Given the pathos of the book, however, it is not at all clear that McNamara has learned anything or has broken with the rationality of technical competence, for at the end he discerns a series of learnings to be used by the next generation of rational certitude.

In a subsequent television interview, McNamara reinforced his pathos with the wistful recognition, "We simply did not know"—a mouthful indeed, deep out of the tradition of modernist certitude rooted in "objective reason." What was not known, and could not be known in such a given of autonomous reason, concerned the power, energy, and resilience of tradition-rooted, land-loving societies that are immune to the "givenness" of imperial force. All of which is to say that the givenness of such reason, all over the West, when pushed to its anxious extremity, has been a given of simple, uncriticized power, inattentive to the irreducible givenness of the human. There is no need to denigrate the great good of this given, for it brought with it enormous emancipation. But when settled, unchallenged, and made into a mode of control, its emancipatory impulses have been overrun by its sheer power.

3. In this quick summary of givenness, altogether too sweeping, it is now possible to suggest a new hegemonic given that has come abruptly behind The Age of Reason. Until we see it more clearly, it may be dubbed "the Age of Information." Its prophet is perhaps Francis Fukuyama who, since 1989 and the collapse of the Soviet Union, has gloated over the ultimate and irreversible triumph of liberal capitalism, the final elimination of any sustainable challenge to capitalism as a total, defining force in the world.[9] Of course, there are deep continuities between the old claims of the Enlightenment and the new modes of capital globalization. But they are also very different,

for the Bill Gates phenomenon is not explicitly committed to the old dogmas of settled reason. Now everything is reduced to technical capacity; any question, moreover, that does not admit of surface response is sure to be a dismissed question. The difference from the older Reason may be that such simplistic technological perception is a "dumbing down." Nevertheless, this givenness shares with its antecedents a totalism that is intolerant of any who are not "with the program," including those who, for reasons of context, have no chance to "get with" the program. The outcome would seem to be an incredible thinning of human questions and human possibilities.

Now, this rapid naming of medieval synthesis, Enlightenment rationality, and contemporary computerism is much too simplistic; and if simplistic, perhaps pretentious on my part, though I do not claim to know or understand all that is implied in this naming. My point is a simple one, that these sequenced givens are, as much as possible, totalizing, closed to newness, and resistant to criticism. Each in turn, moreover, comes to touch and shape the most elemental realities of human community and human personhood; they are therefore of primal concern to the Christian tradition with its tense, questioning relationship to every totalizing given. Such givenness characteristically thins the human spirit, makes hope lean, and saps the energy required for daring obedience.[10]

Making Room for Otherwise

The Christian tradition broadly and the Reformed tradition in particular—with its resilient impulse toward "otherwise"—can give thanks for the fact that in recent times this interpretive tradition has important allies in the emergence of modern/postmodern hermeneutics, which characteristically challenges any flat, one-dimensional notion of the given. The rise of hermeneutical awareness has permitted alternative ways of knowing that are not easily dismissed by and that refuse to accept the settled givens, whether they are doctrinal, rational, or technical.

1. By the 1950s, *Michael Polanyi* had begun to articulate an awareness that scientific learning is fundamentally a fiduciary operation that depends upon trust among researchers and therefore has an intrinsic, defining *personal* element.[11] That is, all knowledge is in some sense an interpretive act, so that we never deal simply with raw data or "facts"

that are the same regardless of the stance of the observer.[12] The introduction of the personal, interpretive, subjective element into knowledge of course undermines any thin notion of certitude, scientific, technological, or theological.

2. Polanyi's work was dramatically reinforced in 1962 when *Thomas Kuhn* wrote his spectacular book *The Structure of Scientific Revolutions*.[13] Put in over-simple fashion, it is Kuhn's argument that scientific learning does not advance incrementally by the steady accumulation of data, but by the emergence of new interpretive paradigms that drastically rearrange data. The emergence of new interpretive modes, moreover, is characteristically a *novum*, an act of brilliant hunch, of insight, of inspiration, of imagination, whereby a scholar breaks with well-established domain assumptions. The impact of Kuhn's work is inevitably controversial among scientists, but its suggestion cannot be undone. For our purposes, it is important to learn from Kuhn that knowledge is shaped—inescapably—by shrewd and compelling acts of imagination, around which data can be organized in profoundly alternative ways.

3. Closer to our own work, the contribution of *Alasdair MacIntyre* brings thinking like that of Polanyi and Kuhn to the work of theological adjudication.[14] MacIntyre has argued that ethical thinking is never "objective," that is, a flat, obvious given, but it is always embedded in a large narrative account of reality. MacIntyre proposes that we may identify *three rival accounts* of reality in which ethics can be embedded, which he designates as Aristotle, Encyclopedia, Genealogy. It is, moreover, obvious that embeddedness in any of these yields a very different ethic. It is MacIntyre's insistence that there is no ethic outside of an interpretive tradition, which in turn means that there is no thin rationality able to deliver an ethic. Every ethic presupposes an embeddedness.

4. *Charles Taylor*, in his exhaustive study *Sources of the Self*, has made a complementary argument that the self is never an autonomous agent, but is always an agent embedded in and generated by an interpretive tradition.[15] That is, the self is never "given," but is "summoned" in a concrete context.

The contributions of Polanyi, Kuhn, MacIntyre, and Taylor have the profound effect of making us aware that it could be *otherwise* than we think it to be in our dominant modes of certitude and perception. It could be otherwise, and "otherwise" undermines and subverts every absolute claim, including those now made in thin, technical certitude that purports to float above serious commitment.

The Burden of Otherwise

It is my urging then, that imagination—the liberated capacity to picture (image) reality in alternative ways outside conventional, commonly accepted givens—represents the capacity and willingness to host "otherwise" and the actual practice of otherwise. The recognition of an available otherwise, whenever it is taken seriously, ought rightly to make us uneasy with our unexamined givens even if logically secure or experientially established, because every settlement—doctrinal, national, technological—is to some extent an act of interpretation that is itself shot through with imaginative power. Even "givens" begin in imaginative construal.

This act of imagination that inescapably constitutes our knowledge—including our scientific and our theological certitudes—acknowledges that our life in the world is not simple or flat or thin or easy or obvious; it is, rather, laden with interpretive potential that is not exhausted at first glance. More specifically, imagination is hosted in the awareness that in, with, and under our settlements and assurances there live deep measures of ambiguity, hyperbole, incongruity, contradiction, impossibility that always break into possibility—all the powers of untamedness that we hope to tame or keep invisible by our certitudes.

It is my insistence about this otherwise that

a. This otherwise is the substance that has preoccupied the *"masters of suspicion"* who have resisted Enlightenment thinness (Marx, Nietzsche, and Freud) and the *deconstructionists* (Derrida, Foucault, and Levinas) who understand that official certitudes in the modern West to some great extent live a lie.[16]

b. This otherwise is the "stuff" of human existence that now breaks out all around us in shrillness, the voice of the silenced now speaking, the rage of the unnoticed, the incivility of the excluded, the brutality of those who are deep into despair, but also the lyrical assertion of those driven and summoned to healed futures that stand in judgment on our present. In the face of such eruptions beyond reason, our conventional modes of control are helpless.

c. This deep otherwise—note well *deep*—is best articulated, as the rabbis and midrashic traditions understood, in the playfulness of a biblical text that refuses thin certitude, culminating, perhaps, in the depth-insights of Freud and all his derivative company.[17]

d. This forceful otherwise is peculiarly entrusted to *church and synagogue, to ministers and rabbis*, who have the most remarkable access both to the text and to human stuff, whose work depends upon thinking and speaking otherwise of a reality that cannot be acknowledged or tamed or contained by any thin certitude of doctrine, relativity, or technology.

What happens in this awareness of rooted imagination is that the established reasonableness of modernity and the thin technique of postmodernity are now powerfully *deprivileged,* and the totalism of technology is seen to be less than total. We are able to see that at bottom the matter of knowing is not in the givenness, for example, of rational males and rational whites against "hysterical women" and "shrill blacks"; in fact, our struggle for certitude is a matter of contestation between competing acts of imagination, some of which tilt to management and some of which tilt to emancipation and the hosting of the impossible; but no *a priori* privilege is given to acts of imagination that have become established givens. While both sorts of imagination—managerial and emancipatory—are present in the Bible, the great force of the Bible, culminating in the parables of Jesus and in the impossible claim of Easter, is on the side of emancipation that "managed care" cannot tolerate.[18]

It will be evident as I draw closer to the biblical text that I am speaking not only of competing modes of *knowledge,* but also of competing modes of *rhetoric,* because what we *say* is what we *get.*[19] The point is an important one and comes down, in the practice of the church, to the enigmatic relationship between *knowledge* (reality) and *rhetoric* (speech). It is evident that where the emancipated rhetoric of the Bible occurs, it refuses to submit to old givens, but simply explodes in daring offers of a new reality that emerges in and with the very utterance. It is my judgment that much of our church rhetoric is tamed away from "otherwise," either by *scholastic reduction* or by *historical criticism*, to be sure that the Bible issues in nothing subversive. The struggle for faithful rhetoric in the church is a powerful case in point of the stunning analysis of John D. O'Banion's *Reorienting Rhetoric.*[20] O'Banion organizes the history of Western rhetoric into what he calls "list" and "story." "List" features among others Plato, Descartes, and the dismissal of rhetoric in the twentieth century. But these "lists" are only intrusions into the power of "story," by which he means the narrative articulation about the density of human life. It is O'Banion's burden to show that the "demise of narrative" culminates in *anomie*, because human life cannot survive on or be sustained by autonomous logic that no longer embodies human "thickness" that resists logic.[21]

Enacting Otherwise

I want now to consider a formidable biblical offer of the tension of settled givens and the enactment of otherwise, of *list and story*, in order to show a way in which the Bible advocates and insists upon the hosting of otherwise. I take as my model the books of First and Second Kings. As is well known, this material is essentially a fairly boring, predictable summary account of the kings of Israel and Judah that we Christians commonly label as "history." After Solomon, the recital is seemingly endless, about birth, capital city, mother, age, length of reign, death, place of burial, and verdict. There are, to be sure, variations dictated by particular circumstance, but these several elements account for the primary line of presentation.

What interests us now, however, is the odd intrusion into "Kings" of the narratives of Elijah (1 Kings 17—21; 2 Kings 1—2) and Elisha (2 Kings 2—13).[22] These narratives clearly interrupt the regularized formulation of royal power and are given to us in a very different mode of expression. Moreover, they occupy about one-third of the books of Kings and in fact function not only to disrupt but also to call into question the significance of the royal account of reality. I shall urge that these prophetic narratives are indeed "story" against "list." They are acts of imagination against settled, controlled certitudes, an offer of otherwise in the midst of royal administration. Moreover, they are an enactment of otherwise in both their historical occurrence (whatever that was) and in their canonical recurrence, inviting the ongoing canonical community to host otherwise in its own time and place through repeated, attentive hearing. The stories, unlike the royal list, open to the listeners in daring imagination the claim that the world does not need to be perceived or engaged according to dominant shapings of power, to privileged notions of authority, to conventional distributions of goods, or to standard definitions of what is possible.

Let me mention some obvious dimensions of otherwise in the Elijah narratives:

1. The prophet does not depend upon normal food supplies and will accept no junk food from the king. He is from the outset a resister (1 Kings 17:1–7). He is otherwise than a conventional character who takes royal guarantees of sustenance as a given.

2. He is a source of plenty in a world defined by scarcity (1 Kings 17:8–16). He is the one who comes to the widow of Zarephath, to one fated by social power to be destitute and vulnerable, and assures her of ongoing, reliable sustenance:

> For thus says the LORD the God of Israel: "The jar of meal will not be emptied and the jug of oil will not fail until the day that the LORD sends rain on the earth."...The jar of meal was not emptied, neither did the jug of oil fail, according to the word of the LORD that he spoke by Elijah. (1 Kings 17:14, 16)

Elijah is otherwise than the usual calculus of deathly scarcity in a world of royal monopoly.

3. He is the source of life in a world where death is taken to be final (1 Kings 17:17–24). He does this amazing act of revitalization—an earnest of Easter!—by prayer:

> "O LORD my God, have you brought calamity even upon the widow with whom I am staying, by killing her son?...LORD my God, let this child's life come into him again" (vv. 20–21).

In his first prayer, Elijah dares to suggest that Yahweh has treated the widow like everyone else has treated her. The prayer of Elijah causes a *novum* in the life of the widow, who is not privy to much newness. She must respond:

"Now I know that you are a man of God, and that the word of the LORD in your mouth is truth" (v. 24).

Imagine! Life wrought for a widow in the face of death! Elijah is otherwise than all those who succumb impotently to the Last Enemy.

4. He is "a troubler of Israel" (1 Kings 18:17). But of course this verdict is on the lips of the king. Elijah does not trouble *all* of Israel; rather, he troubles royal, settled, entrenched Israel. He has not respected present power arrangements and enacts a power outside what is taken to be legitimate. His is a political act, as the king rightly perceives. But a political act is always a theological act as well. Elijah takes on the gods of Ahab and Jezebel, causes a showdown at Carmel. He defeats the prophets of Baal even as Yahweh defeats Baal. He exposes the sexual mysteries of Baalism as fraudulent. Elijah is otherwise than all those who get along by going along with consensus arrangements.

5. He is the king's "enemy" (1 Kings 21:20). Everyone thought that the story of Naboth's vineyard had ended in v. 16 when Naboth was executed and Ahab secured the coveted land. But the narrator hangs around after the royal gain is established. He hangs around to see what else will happen. He warns us, do not leave in the seventh inning! The text says "Then" (v. 17). Then Yahweh sent Elijah. *Then* the story begins. It does not begin until this enactor of "otherwise" is onstage. And *then* comes the threat to the royal family, an act of high treason:

> "Because you have sold yourself to do what is evil in the sight of the LORD, I will bring disaster on you; I will consume you, and will cut off from Ahab every male, bond or free, in Israel; and I will make your house like the house of Jeroboam son of Nebat, and like the house of Baasha son of Ahijah, because you have provoked me to anger and have caused Israel to sin. Also concerning Jezebel the LORD said, 'The dogs shall eat Jezebel within the bounds of Jezreel.' Anyone belonging to Ahab who dies in the city the dogs shall eat; and anyone of his who dies in the open country the birds of the air shall eat." (1 Kings 21:20–24)

There must have been a long pause after this speech. How dare he say such things! We must honor the speech of "otherwise" in the face of the king by a long pause every time we read it. Indeed, for ten chapters we pause, because imagination does not issue in instant reality. The speech lingers and haunts as we wait. We wait and do not know, as communities that relish and treasure imagination characteristically wait and do not know. There is waiting and not knowing until 2 Kings 9:36–37:

> "This is the word of the LORD, which he spoke by his servant Elijah the Tishbite, 'In the territory of Jezreel the dogs shall eat the flesh of Jezebel; the corpse of Jezebel shall be like dung on the field in the territory of Jezreel, so that no one can say, This is Jezebel.'"

Elijah—big interruption ="Yahweh is my God"—is a problem for the king, a hope for the poor, a dazzlement in Israel that no one can decode. The story is so improbable that it is hard to take with seriousness. Biblical critics—all of us tempted by Descartes—take the texts "light." They are, since Gunkel, "legends"—not real, could not have happened, not as real as the royal lists.[23] Such reluctance on our part, however, does not intimidate or impede Elijah. He just keeps at his dangerous, God-given imagination, making all things new. He enacts otherwise, showing that the world could be and would be different, concretely, decisively different.

I do not know about "historicity" here, nor does anyone else. But canonical imagination worries only a little about "historicity." In his parables, Jesus later said, "It is as if…" and we entertain the "as if" as our true context for life.[24] I do not know about historicity, but I do know about canonicity. I know that this stuff made it into the Bible. Our fathers and mothers judged the material worth keeping, worth knowing, and worth hearing…over and over. Whatever is "historicity," we find ourselves addressed by this inexplicable enactor of "otherwise," recognizing that such otherwise is always inexplicable.

If this enactment of otherwise made it into our sacred scriptures, we must ask, then what are we supposed to hear when we hear these words? It strikes us as we listen that this imaginative material generates futures as royal lists could never do. So try this:

• When we hear the recital of Elijah, we are supposed to remember that the Christian Old Testament ends in Malachi 4:5–6 in this way:

> Lo, I will send you the prophet Elijah before the great and terrible day of the LORD comes. He will turn the hearts of

parents to their children and the hearts of children to their parents, so that I will not come and strike the land with a curse.

Elijah will be back. And when he comes back, he will reconcile parents and children. He will enact "family values" so there will be no curse. He will enact what the world thinks is impossible.

• When we hear the recital of Elijah, we are supposed to remember that the ongoing, still living character of Elijah hovered powerfully around the life of Jesus:

John the Baptist: "He is Elijah who is to come. Let anyone with ears listen" (Mt. 11:14).

Who do people say: "Some say...Elijah" (Mt. 16:14).

At the mountain: Suddenly there appeared to them Moses and Elijah, talking with him (Mt. 17:3).

At the cross: "This man is calling for Elijah" (Mt. 27:47).

When the early church pondered Jesus, cadences of Elijah rang in their ears, because they sensed that Jesus was an enactment of a dangerous, healing, liberating otherwise that could not be stopped. And they remembered the earlier time when they had come face-to-face with otherwise.

Elijah is profoundly in the midst of the story of Jesus, the old otherwise in the new, embodied otherwise. Like Elijah before him, Jesus is not credible to the authorities. And even if the two of them are not connected in other ways, they are bound in an emerging otherwise in ways that defy royal reason and call into question the entire royal arrangement.

Thus, the angel announcement to Elizabeth about the son to be born, John, at the break of newness, must allude to Elijah:

"With the spirit and power of Elijah he will go before him, to turn the hearts of parents to their children, and the disobedient to the wisdom of the righteous, to make ready a people prepared for the Lord" (Lk. 1:17).

Mark, moreover, surely understood, when he retold the raising of the daughter of Jairus, that he was retelling Elijah, now redeployed by imagination to Jesus:

When he had entered, he said to them, "Why do you make a commotion and weep? The child is not dead but sleeping." And they laughed at him. Then he put them all outside, and took the child's father and mother and those who were with them, and went in where the child was. He took her by the hand and said to her, "Talitha cum," which means, "Little girl, get up!" And immediately the girl got up and began to walk about...At this they were overcome with amazement. (Mk. 5:39–42)

The whole collage of otherwise defies the way the world is, and sets the watching, listening community into a dangerous, alternative life, an alternative not even visible as long as we stay with the settled story line of the kings.

• When we hear the recital of Elijah, we are supposed to name the names of the *carriers of otherwise* who are closer at hand, who keep reflowing the juices of possibility. We have names in common and we each have our own inventory:

o Clarence Jordan, who defied racism in America,
o Mother Teresa, who defied poverty for the sake of life,
o Nelson Mandela, who did not grow weary or cynical,
o Eugene Debs, who insisted that public power must serve real people,
o Martin Luther King, who dreamed beyond hate and lingers even now with power,
o Frederick Douglass and W. E. B. DuBois and Malcolm X, none of whom could make a difference, but did, and were commonly thought to be both "Troubler" and "Enemy."

The phrasing conjures and makes available all these who thought otherwise and who, like Elisha in the train of Elijah, noticed the mountains covered with friendly horses and friendly chariots and friendly resources that the king could neither discern nor control (2 Kings 6:14–17).

• When we hear the recital of Elijah, we are authorized to reconstrue our own lives out beyond the closed definitions we have too long inhaled, definitions given us by well-meaning parents, and by brutalizing siblings, and by careless teachers who have flattened and boxed and caged until we are trapped in our own royal list,

capable only of being good,

only of being angry,

only of being obedient,

only of being lustful and greedy,

capable of only, only…

And then comes the gift of otherwise—call it Easter, call it resurrection—and we notice that on an attentive day we, like these ancients, are overcome with amazement at the gift of new life in the land of otherwise. Of course, all the flatteners from Ahab to Descartes to Fukuyama would not notice; and if they noticed, they would think the newness is a trick and not a newness. Elijah, however, never gives in to such cynical dismissiveness, but goes on into the land of possibility—even now.

The Marks of Otherwise

My theme is the practice of imagination entrusted to us in the church, a capability of otherwise so deep in our call, so urgent in our context, so dangerous in our practice.

1. This practice of imagination is *textual.* It arises from the intense and sustained study of this inexhaustible text that we take to be Holy Scripture. We notice regularly that this text comprises for us and offers to us what is not otherwise known. This text-driven, text-compelled imagination keeps us under the discipline of close study, for it is not free-lance fantasy.[25] The matter of the text is urgent, precisely because a "modernist" church—liberal and conservative—has largely given up on the text as our gospel script of otherwise.

2. This practice of imagination is *sacramental.* Of course, I refer chiefly to baptism and eucharist, for it is always "Word and Sacrament." We find in the grace-filled practice of water and wine and bread that these acts ripple with possibility we have been too dulled to notice; indeed, people sometimes notice what we have missed in our familiarity. At the same time, I mean, beyond the two sacraments, our larger awareness that all our common practices in the community of faith are coded and loaded and freighted in density, all of life invested

with holy otherwise, sometimes voiced, often only signaled, giving a world well outside the royal recital, outside where visible power is operative, and food is shared, and lives are raised to newness we know not how.

This practice of imagination is *ecclesial* in its intention. That is, it intends to summon, evoke, and form an alternative community. It is not romantic in terms of private address to autonomous individuals who may be uncommonly responsive, but aims to offer a community in touch with its own odd identity and its own odd purpose in the world, to live into and out of the freedom evoked in this counter-construal.

This practice of imagination is *ethical* in its passion.[26] It summons those taken by its offer to a radical and enduring commitment, articulated in concrete neighbor acts that are dangerous, done simply because we refuse to conform to dominant royal imagination.

This practice of imagination is *oppositional* in its stance, clearly offering an account of reality that is deeply contrasted with dominant imagination that is too much taken as a given. Such an oppositional stance may be enacted in many ways and need not always be one of direct confrontation. It may be nothing more than a determined refusal to accept the mandates and limits set by other acts of imagination, a resolve to proceed according to this construal of reality, without bothering to confront or refute what it opposes.

I finish with two conclusions. The first is this. I am in fact not proposing something new. I am rather naming what we do pastorally, homiletically, and liturgically in more or less haphazard ways all the time. In truth, if one examines the great hymns and prayers or the sacramental cadences of the church, it is abundantly clear that the characteristic rhetoric of the church, when it speaks its own "mother tongue," is in images and metaphors and narratives and songs and oracles that make almost no concession to dominant definitions of the possible. What is fresh in current conversation is the awareness that, at the end of modernity and at the end of Christian domination, imagination is a valued mode of knowledge, that such knowledge is not subject to the tests of dominant modes of certitude, and that it may be found on the lips and in the utterances of strangely excluded, uncredentialed, seemingly irrational folk, folk not unlike Elijah.

Second, there are those who are very nervous about imagination, for it is taken (mistakenly) to be an act of autonomous fantasy in which an individual person makes claims of the sort that "anything goes."[27] But of course that is not what is meant in this discussion. It means, rather, to let the Bible, its words and its claims, make contact with the life-and-death issues of our own time and place, contact not originally intended in the text, and contact that is not obvious or visible except by daring acts of reconstrual. Richard B. Hays has made the point well in his recent analysis of New Testament ethics:

> I suggested above that in order to practice New Testament ethics as a normative theological discipline, we will have to formulate imaginative *analogies* between the stories told in the text and the story lived out by our community in a very different historical setting…the use of the New Testament in normative ethics requires *an integrative act of the imagination*, a discernment about how our lives…might fitly answer to that narration and participate in the truth that it tells…*Whenever we appeal to the authority of the New Testament, we are necessarily engaged in metaphor-making, placing our community's life imaginatively within the world articulated by the texts.*[28]

Such an act of imaginative construal out beyond any flat surface reading is what we do intuitively when we read scripture well and responsibly.[29] In the end it is possible to understand such an enterprise as spirit-led reading, inspired reading. That is a legitimate transposition of the point argued here, as long as we recognize the mandate of emancipated thought on the part of the interpretive community, and as long as we understand that this is the work of rhetoric, the liberation to re-utter afresh what is given us in the text that refuses the sanctions of the dominant world.

Such an enterprise requires of most of the church's interpreters a great deal of unlearning about scripture, unlearning the claims made for casting scripture in dogmatic formulation, unlearning about historical critical claims that serve to discount what is interpretively most demanding in the text. It is likely that our best models for such interpretation are to be found precisely in the churches of the marginalized, among those not excessively schooled in modernity. Much of the church in the West has been well schooled in resistance to otherwise. The task we have and the context in which we live now require "otherwise," available only in the daring capacity to picture and enact afresh. It is not too late to leave an empty chair for Elijah at Passover—or at Easter—or almost any time. Neither dogmatic certitude, nor historical critical flatness, nor technological thinness has been able to eliminate him from our future. If we forgo his impossible presence, we are left with only the mantras of the royal list. That, of course, is not our true birthright.

3

Miracle and Accommodation

The Story of a Military Man (2 Kings 5:1–27)

On the basis of a quite general "either/or" and in terms of the "otherwise" of Elijah, I want now to draw closer to a specific text. For it is finally in specific texts that the truth is told to which we must pay attention.

Characters

I take up the narrative of 2 Kings 5, which divides into two parts: vv. 1–19a, a healing narrative, and vv. 19b–27, a narrative of negative reversal. The story occurs in the midst of the Elijah cycle of narratives that scholars are wont to term "legends," a term that means that the narrative violates our sense of the possible, and therefore we do not really believe in its "happenedness."[1] Since his empowerment in 2:13–14 when he received the mantle of Elijah, Elisha is a character in the memory and imagination of Israel who is larger than life. He already has been a public figure in the military venture of Israel in chapter 3, and in chapter 4, in rapid succession he has supplied oil to a poverty-stricken widow so that she would not be devoured by her creditors (vv. 1–7), he has given a son to the Shunemite woman who wanted a son and had none (vv. 8–17), he has raised the dead son of that same woman (vv. 18–37), he has purified a pot of stew (vv. 38–41), and he has fed a hundred hungry people and had food left over (vv. 42–44). In all of these acts, he is a wonder worker who has refused the given world that has left his people needful, in jeopardy, and under threat.[2] In all five acts of rescue already committed by the prophet, Elisha has summoned inexplicable powers to enact transformative turns toward life that conventional givenness had precluded in principle.

It is no wonder that in 8:46 this inexplicable character has come to the attention of the king in Samaria, Jehu by name. The king engages Gehazi, an aide to Elisha: "Tell me about Elisha." Tell me, *sipperah-nah*, a narrative or two. Tell me about his "great things" (*gedolôth*), tell me about the things out of the ordinary, because a king would not inquire about the ordinary. Perhaps the king is only interested; perhaps he is pleased to think he has such a subject in his realm. Or perhaps he sees the prophet as a threat, commanding power that even the king cannot curb. The answer of the aide is to cite the most spectacular case, the resurrection of the dead boy. Gehazi narrates a quite concrete Easter when this enigmatic, unapproachable character summons life out of death.

The General

Given such a torrent of testimony offered by the narrator, and given the notice taken by the king in Samaria, it is not surprising that the general in Syria also noticed the prophet. The very telling of the story contains high irony, for Syria is the sworn enemy of Israel, has been for a long while in the books of Kings (even as the unsettled issue of the Golan Heights continues to keep it so now). For that reason, it is odd that Israel should be on the personal map of the Syrian general as a place of healing. What Syrian needs Israel for healing?

But of course the general has special needs, and special needs cause us to do things our neighbors would never approve. The general is celebrated by the narrator with three positive terms. He is a "great man," at root the same Hebrew term used to characterize Elisha's miracles, *gedolôth* (8:4). We move with him in the zone of greatness. He is in "high favor" with his king, that is, the king has "lifted his face," has noticed him, and likely has given him a special medal (see Gen. 40:20). He has "won a great victory" for Syria. He is indeed a "mighty warrior" (*gibbôr hayil*), a mighty man of valor upon whom the order, stability, and security of the realm depend. This is a medal of honor winner, surely at home in high places, by this time a "political general" with access to seats of power. He has by now become accustomed to perks, privileges, and advantages. He is indeed a celebrity. Our cunning narrator slips in a little hint of things to come. Not that he won a victory, rather, "Because of him Yahweh had given victory to Syria." He is, though he does not know it, an agent of Yahweh. He is one of Karl Rahner's "anonymous Christians," an "anonymous Israelite," doing the bidding of the God of Israel, all the while thinking he is only a good Syrian military man.

He has, however, a problem, a deep problem upon which the entire story turns. He has leprosy![3] There is no speculation on how he contracted the dread disease. It is in any case serious, even defining. It is a most dangerous, despicable social disease that made him quickly, as we say, "a leper." He was surely *persona non grata* for all of the lively places of access to which he had previously gained entry. The verdict "He is unclean," a simple two-word verdict, is a quick and drastic negation of all the positive characterization we have reviewed from v. 1. End of his career, end of influence, end of prestige, end! He is about to become an invisible nobody. He must have wept in the night even while he put on a brave face in public.

He goes to seek help. He has heard there is help in Israel. He goes, even though it is something of a scandal for a Syrian to seek Israelite help. But such a desperate condition causes one to do scandalous, awkward, unthinkable things. He receives permission from his king, here nameless, who sends a letter of introduction to the king of Israel, because kings deal only with other kings. The general, moreover, comes to Samaria, brings not only his leprosy with him, but also ten talents of silver, 6000 shekels of gold, and ten sets of garments. He is no charity case. He comes bearing gifts, or a bribe; he comes prepared to pay well for the best available health care, no doubt anticipating a private, luxurious room for his period of confinement. Likely the "ten sets of garments" are also an expensive gift. It occurred to me, however, that perhaps he planned to dress for dinner and carry on some visible social life, this military man with a social disease.

But of course, it is all a big mistake, an upsetting mistake. The general comes with an impressive entourage; he brings a royal letter of introduction to the Israelite king, but this second king is appalled at his approach to his city. The king in Samaria is no healer. He has no cure for leprosy. He thinks he is being put on the spot, embarrassed;

perhaps the approach from Syria is meant to be provocative, because Syria tries always to provoke Israel. This is no different from always. What a mismatch, a king and a disease, but kings have no power to heal. Just in passing, the narrative of Kings continues its relentless exposé of royal figures as decorated irrelevance. The two kings and the general are mutually impressed with each other. None of it, however, counts for anything.

The general makes a second effort, swallowing pride, comes now to Elisha, the real subject of the narrative. The general arrives at the house of Elisha, no doubt a modest, even humble place compared to royal Samaria; the general arrives, as generals will, with horses and chariots. The arrival is rather like an entourage of military limousines arriving in a peasant village. Everybody gawks. The general again has great expectations. He wants a big, dramatic healing, even if it is not to be royal:

> "I thought that for me he would surely come out, and stand and call on the name of the LORD his God, and would wave his hand over the spot, and cure the leprosy!" (v. 11).

Obviously he has been watching too much television. The prophetic health care strategy, however, is quite low key. The prophet does not even come out to meet the great man. He only sends an LPN out with a prescription:

> "Go, wash in the Jordan seven times, and your flesh shall be restored and you shall be clean" (v. 10).

The general wants something dramatic, something scientific, technical, expensive; but he gets only this, only a river washing, rather like a needy Anglican receiving a low-brow Baptist remedy; moreover, such a pitiful little river, the Jordan. The general is indignant that the healer will not match his status with attentiveness. The general knows bigger, better rivers back home. He senses that he is being humiliated— perhaps as Israelites always want to do to Syrians, perhaps as prophets always want to do to kings and their generals. In any case, this man is deeply needy, but he will not crawl in humiliation. "He turned and went away in a rage." End of effort.

This second effort at healing turned out no better than the first try with the king. Just at the last moment, the servants of the general prevail on him to try the simple little folk remedy:

"Father, if the prophet had commanded you to do something difficult, would you not have done it? How much more, when all he said to you was, 'Wash, and be clean'?" (v. 13).

The general goes reluctantly, grudgingly to the Jordan. He submits. He is not used to submitting...and he is healed! He receives what the rivers of Syria would never yield. He receives what the king of Samaria could not grant. He is fully restored.

He is, moreover, grateful. He did not know, back in verse 1, that it had been Yahweh who had given him victory. He did not know (not being a Calvinist) that God had been at work his whole long life to bring him to this moment of wholeness and gratitude. And so he says:

"Now I know that there is no God in all the earth except in Israel" (v. 15).

A Syrian doxology to the God of Israel! The general knows enough, in the supple hands of the narrator, to look beyond the prophet who heals to the God of the prophet. Yahweh is the one who finally manages the Jordan and its healing capacities.

But immediately after the doxology to Yahweh, in the same voice, the general reverts to military procedure. He is back in role: "Please accept a present from your servant...No, really, let me pay. I am able to pay and do not need charity. I would rather it were a transaction than a gift." This last little offer is a characteristic attempt to recover from the humiliation of being reduced to a recipient of a folk remedy. The Syrian general tries to draw the healing into the arena of commerce where he is more comfortable and competent. But he cannot. The general moves from leprosy through humiliating submissiveness to wholeness. He moves from leprosy to wholeness, a standard miracle, so standard and normal that we do not easily notice the drama and the wonder...unless we have had leprosy lately.

Elisha

The general, of course, dominates the story, as generals are wont to do. In the end, however, he does not do anything. He only receives. But then, that is the hardest thing for such a prestigious person to do; and he does find it humiliating. Because he is not a primal actor in this account of healing, we must ask, how did this healing happen?

The short answer is, by the gift of Yahweh, as the general himself acknowledges in his doxology to Yahweh in verse 15.

We, however, are interested in the long answer. The long answer of healing, of course, concerns Elisha. He is the healer. The narrative wants to say that this *carrier of Yahweh's transformative power* merits all of our attention. He is indeed a misfit in his own society. He does not live in an alien society, except that every royal-military environment is alien to such a power of transformation, because such societies are organized precisely to resist transformation. Elisha is alien in his society; he is other, totally other, a most "Significant Other" around whom the story revolves. The narrator—and we may believe, along with the ancient account, modern scholarship as well—does not know what to make of him. He does not fit usual categories, this alien, this force from another rootage. For that reason, the narrator offers no explanation for his strange achievement of healing, exhibits no curiosity about him, and makes no generalizations from him. The narrator stays close to the concreteness of a particular moment, the way outsiders must always do.

Elisha appears late in the narrative, only in verse 8, after the royal drama has been played out to a fizzle. Indeed, Elisha is standing by, ready, for he knows the royal effort will fizzle. He is privy to the king's conduct, always keeping a vigilant eye on royal characters. He knows that the Israelite king has torn his clothes in a gesture of exasperation (v. 7). He sends a message to entrenched power: "Cool it…what are you upset about? You have committed this unnecessary, overwrought gesture of attempted healing because you have strayed out of your territory into mine. Your territory is merely visible power, but visible power almost never heals. My turf is healing, and your kind of turf and my kind of turf rarely overlap. Be cool, acknowledge your limitation that you seem to forget when you spend all your time in the illusionary world of kings and generals":

> "Why have you torn your clothes? Let him come to me, that he may learn that there is a prophet in Israel" (v. 8).

There is a prophet in Israel! You have to learn that. You have to learn that there is healing presence, because there is an embodied human force outside of normal channels and you have to learn it. You have to take your savaged body outside the safe environs of your control and submit in trust to my peculiar power.

The prophet is waiting for the general at his house. This is a house call, but the general must make it. The alien voice of the prophet is terse and remote. He does not even come to the door to meet the great man; he sends a messenger. The messenger simplifies: Here's all you need to do; don't bother the busy, great man. It never occurred to the general that this nobody would be too busy for him, but perhaps the drill is in order to indicate that submissiveness is a prerequisite for healing. The message is an imperative; no greeting, no warm-up, no intake interview, no examination: Go wash...seven times...Jordan. Go in obedience. Wash, acknowledging your ritual uncleanness:

Wash yourselves; make yourselves clean;
  remove the evil of your doings
  from before my eyes;
cease to do evil...(Isa. 1:16).

Wash me thoroughly from my iniquity,
  and cleanse me from my sin...
Purge me with hyssop, and I shall be clean;
  wash me, and I shall be whiter than snow (Ps. 51:2, 7).

The washing is a humiliating public act of need. Seven times...only seven; it is the best number, a perfect number, a number of irrationality that defies any controlled agenda. Folk remedies are like that: swing the cat's tail over your head four times and say six times, "Go away cat." Folk numbers are like that: try circling the city seven times and watch it fall. Folk remedies are like that: take two aspirins, not one, not four, call me, let me know. Submit to Israelite practice...trust me and submit. The Jordan. This prophet perhaps had not traveled much, perhaps did not know other rivers; but he knew the Jordan. The Jordan is the boundary. Elisha had been at the Jordan in chapter 2 when Elijah ascended. He had been at the Jordan when he received the mantle and came back to Jericho. He had been at the Jordan when Elijah crossed it to receive his call while he ate raven food. He had been at the Jordan with Joshua when they moved the stones and crossed over on dry land. He will be at the Jordan with Hosea when Yahweh takes Israel back over to the Valley Trouble to woo and create "a door of hope." He will be at the Jordan when the Baptizer comes storming in about repentance and forgiveness. He will be at the Jordan when the dove-like voice says, "This is the One." He will be at the Jordan when Michael rows his boat ashore.

Do I overstate and claim too much? My point is that this alien one carries his map and his terrain and his historical geography all in his memory, and can activate it and appeal to it in every strange place. He does not need a degree in the geography of Syrian rivers and he does not need honoraria to navigate the river. The Jordan is a freighted, loaded place that in this simplicity mediates the very possibilities of Yahweh that the royal-military world believes to be impossible. His offer of healing is a sacrament not credible to those who live on commodity every day.

The double imperative, the faith number, the river, all of that in five Hebrew words that hold the future:

Go, wash in the Jordan seven times, and you shall be clean.

Two promises are made to the general: "Your flesh will be restored, you shall be clean." You will be healed. You will be made again socially acceptable. You will be permitted reentry. You as you were; you as you want to be. Five words from inside the house to outside the house, brought by a messenger with two imperatives, two promises, no explanation. Utterance that shattered the aplomb of the general and that puts all our certitude at risk. That is the total appearance of Elisha and his complete work for that day. All the rest of verses 11–14 is an interaction between an enraged, humiliated military man and his wise, patient advisors. Finally, in verse 14, four verses after the prophetic prescription, the general goes. He submits "according to the man of God." In the very next word, nothing between, instantly, the text says:

His flesh was restored like the flesh of a young boy, and he was clean (v. 14).

Restore...flesh...clean! The promise is true. The miracle is complete. And the prophet as an outsider never even got up out of his chair to do it. No wonder the king in Samaria in 8:4 had heard of Elisha's "great things"! Good news travels fast, not only a gift of healing but a gift of healing that in its very enactment overcame a humiliating submission by the Syrian general. Double good news...good news for everyone, worked by the outsider.

The Young Girl

But look closer. The short answer to the question of healing is Yahweh. It is noteworthy that in the prophetic directive of verse 10 or in the narrative report of success of verse 14, Yahweh is not even mentioned as an actor. The short version is so short that Yahweh is only implied. The longer version revolves around the prophet, of course. There is, however, yet an even longer version about this healing. One might have thought that all the healing was in Israel, where both Yahweh and Elisha operated. But there is an earlier point in the story that we must not miss. In verse 2, back in Damascus, just as the narrator has celebrated and then diagnosed the military man, there is a footnote. There is a "young girl" in the story. She is an Israelite held by the Syrians as a prisoner of war.[4] She has been captured by the Syrians in one of their many brutal raids into Israel. She has been brought back to Damascus as war booty. We do not know from where in Israel. We do not know her age or how long she has been in Syria. We do not know her name. She is "young." We do not know how long, how old when captured, how old now. We do not know how she was treated by the Syrians, but we can imagine that she was likely "used" and then made available for housework. All we know is that she is from Israel. Perhaps that is all *she* knew.

For the purposes of our narrative, however, she knew everything she needed to know. She is included in the account of the miracle because she knew and she remembered. She is presented as a docile, obedient servant, a housemaid to the wife of the general, who is herself a *gibborah*, a female *gibbôr*, a woman of substance and force and power. That woman of force and power, however, has no word of healing with which to respond to her needy, frantic husband. She has no useful response to her husband's diagnosis of leprosy. Perhaps—we do not know—she loved the good life of commodity as much as did he, and such a life, we know, permits no useful response in the face of leprosy. Indeed, in the entire story, his wife never speaks. Leprosy has reduced the *gibborah* to silence.

The only one who speaks usefully is the "young girl" (*na'arah qatannah*). She is alien to Damascus, an outsider to Syria, never belonging, never valued, never safe there. She dares to speak. She is able to speak because she remembers. She is required to speak because she knows. She knows what must now be said in Syria that no Syrian knows to say. She speaks wistfully out of her old memory and her deep rootage that years of humiliating servitude have not obliterated. Wistfully—"Oh that, would that, if only"—subjunctive, contrary to fact. If only the Syrian had an Israelite prophet, life in the Israelite zone would trump the Syrian leprosy. The wistfulness is an act of hope, an affirmation of a genuine possibility that is not on the screen of the Syrian who takes leprosy as a dead-end with no healing option. Her statement is an act of hope because she wishes well for her captor. This little utterance of a subjunctive occurs in only one other place, also hope-filled, in Psalm 119:5:

> O that my ways may be steadfast
>   in keeping your statutes!

It is a hoped-for but deeply unlikely option, held only in hope that defies all the evidence. If only I could obey…If only the Syrians knew about Israel.

If only—but the general will not—if only this Syrian were in Israel. There is a prophet there. The young Israelite knows. She remembers. She trusts, she asserts, she declares data against the closed Syrian world where she is held captive. She is a witness to an alternative. She is an evangelist pointing to the one with power. She speaks to the wife of the general.

That is all. The next thing we see is that the general is seeking permission from his king to go to Israel. We are not told that the woman told her husband about the prophet in Israel, that the *gibborah* passed the word to the *gibbôr*. But she must have. Both the powerful woman and the powerful man are being led to new life by this fragile Israelite witness who has not forgotten, and who cannot keep silent in the face of Syrian anguish and pain.

That's it! That is her fifteen minutes of fame, never to come again (really not even fifteen minutes, but only two quick verses). We do not know her name. Fidelity of the sort she embodies does not call attention to itself, and she is not lingered over by the narrative. The Syrians do not thank her or reward her. They do not even remember her. Except that the narrative does remember her, and she is thereby written securely and permanently into this Book of Life where are written the ancestors, the odd ones who remember and tell where the forces of healing can be met.

She never appears again, is never cited, never cross-referenced. Except a hint at the end of our narrative. The prophet said in verse 10, "Your flesh will be restored." But the report of the healing in verse 14 that corresponds to the prophetic promise is slightly modified: "His flesh was restored, like the flesh of a young boy." The promise and the report are exactly parallel:

"Go, wash in the Jordan seven times, and your flesh shall be restored and you shall be clean" (v. 10).

So he went down and immersed himself seven times in the Jordan, according to the word of the man of God; his flesh was restored...and he was clean (v. 14).

The same utterance except for this phrase, "like the flesh of a young boy." The narrator specifies. Leprosy is a skin disease, the skin filled with abrasion, rough, torn, open, unsightly, perhaps with an odor. Now restored. But why "flesh of a young boy"? We are talking about "baby flesh," young, soft, sweet smelling, whole, no flaw, no scar, no abrasion. Why say it in this particular way? Well, because, as commentators have noticed, the phrase "young boy" (*na'ar qaton*) is an exact parallel to the description of the war captive who was a "young girl" (*na'arah qatannah*). If the general had been a woman, the phrase would be the same for both, but allowance must be made in the grammar for gender difference. He is a man, a military man, so the masculine ending. She is a young girl, smooth skin, no abrasion, no foul odor, no leprosy.

And now he has skin just like hers. Of course this is just a casual narrative report, except that among displaced people there are no casual reports. The simple act of healing and the simple report matter. Poets in Czechoslovakia could not be casual, for every word counts. Speakers for newness in Croatia must get every word right. This is not casual narrative. It might be casual to a Syrian reader. The irony in the text, however, is not for a casual Syrian. The irony given in detail is exactly for displaced people who notice what power people do not notice in their summarizing. What we notice is *na'ar qaton* and *na'arah qatannah. He* became like *her.* The Syrian is healed like the Israelite. The great man is healed like the little girl. The big one is healed like the little one. The great Syrian man is healed like the little Israelite girl who remembered and knew and spoke and opened the future by her testimony. The great Syrian man has been humiliated and subverted. He is healed because he submitted to the scandalous agency of the man of God who is filled with strange power. The powers of YHWH are poignant in this story because they are embodied in this prophet. But the powers of the prophet are mobilized in this narrative by the young girl, the one with smooth flesh who invited this brusque man—so full of himself—into the alternative world that seemed to have no force in the alien land of Syria. The young girl was right:

there is a prophet in Israel! The prophet was right: There is healing! The general can go home restored. No wonder he voices a doxology in verse 15!

Praise and Pardon

Now the story ends. The general has sung his doxology to the God of healing, the one reached by the reference of the little girl:

"Now I know that there is no God in all the earth except in Israel" (v. 15).

Then the general offers a present in gratitude and the prophet refuses. The general urges and the prophet refuses a second time. Promptly the general reverses field. Instead of giving, which the prophet will not let him do, he asks. He asks to take two mule-loads of Israelite soil back to Syria as a place in which to offer sacrifices to YHWH, the God of healing. He wants to worship the Israelite God properly on Israelite soil…in Syria. He has just confessed that there is no God in all the earth except in Israel. In his more visceral response, however, he is at stage two in his spiritual development, in what scholars call "henotheism" without the sweeping move to monotheism. But power people are like that; having gotten to power by a series of trade-offs and compromises, they heed many loyalties. It is only "the little ones" who can afford to "will one thing." The general has good intentions in his request to the prophet. The prophet, however, does not answer even to give his permission.

Before the prophet can answer, the general reenters the world of Syrian realism. We can imagine him putting on his Syrian uniform and his servants adjusting his many medals of honor. He is quite aware, yet again, that he really is a Syrian. He has wistful links to the God of Israel, "than whom there is no other"; but he is a Syrian. He immediately reengages his busy, prestigious schedule, and knows he will have to act like a Syrian. He remembers that coming up next month is Veterans Day. He will need to give thanks, on behalf of Syrian veterans, to the gods of Syria. He will be at the head of the liturgical procession and be seated in the front pew in the temple, adding grandeur to the occasion. The television cameras will be on him. He will be there and the liturgy is not to Yahweh but to Rimmon, the god to whom thanks is given in Damascus for all military favors.[5] He trusts the brusque prophet enough to be honest. I am a Syrian.

Or, I must play the role of a Syrian. I will pretend to be yet again a Syrian; if you see me on television in the front pew, you may think I am yet again a Syrian:

> "But may the LORD pardon your servant on one count: when my master goes into the house of Rimmon to worship there, leaning on my arm, and I bow down in the house of Rimmon, when I do bow down in the house of Rimmon, may the LORD pardon your servant on this one count." (v. 18)

Only this one thing, seemingly a huge thing. The general is in a moment of sobering. He knows Yahweh is the only one; but he is a Syrian and must pretend. In verse 18, his Syrian affirmation is framed by "pardon." At the beginning of the verse,

> But may the Lord *pardon* your servant on one count.

At the end of the verse,

> May the Lord *pardon* your servant on this one count.[6]

Pardon me for not being an Israelite. The prophet, as before, is terse: "Go in peace." The prophet does not quibble. There is healing, there is gratitude and acknowledgment. That is enough. The general is given latitude by the prophet to live out his gratitude and his acknowledgment with whatever accommodation he must make. The healing is enough, for the God of Israel has been glorified.[7]

The Servant

That is the end of the story. Except that the narrator adds an addendum in vv. 19b–27, in fact a counter-narrative. Enters now Gehazi, servant of Elisha, about whom we know only in chapter 4. Gehazi, it turns out, has a very different notion of health care delivery. His little, disastrous episode is in three quick scenes over which we linger only briefly:

Scene 1 (vv. 19b–20). Here we are given access to Gehazi's private rumination. He says to himself, "My master has let the Syrian off too lightly, by not accepting the gift he offered." He thinks that perhaps the healing was a free gift, but never turn down a tip. Why not collect something for the free service of the miracle, even though Gehazi has done nothing for the healing?

Scene 2 (vv. 21–25). He goes after the departed general and confronts him. He lies to him about two needy prophets who need a talent of silver and two changes of clothing. It is remarkable that he does not even appeal to the healing but invents a story of need. He is an extortionist. The general, in contrast, is innocent and generous, having a lot for which to be generous. He innocently complies with the phony request of Gehazi and tops it: two changes of clothes as asked, two talents of silver, more than asked. He does not care, because he is grateful. Gehazi takes the larger offer, goes home and hides his gain.

Scene 3 (vv. 25–27). The extortionist must now face the all-knowing prophet. The prophet probes:

"Where have you been?"

The servant lies: "Nowhere."

The prophet exposes the lie:

"Did I not go with you in spirit when someone left his chariot to meet you?" (v. 26).

Gehazi cannot evade this clairvoyant seer: Yes I did! I was there with you all the time. I saw, I know:

"Is this a time to accept money and to accept clothing, olive orchards and vineyards, sheep and oxen, and male and female slaves?" (v. 26).

(Notice the term "accept" from vv. 15, 16, 20, 23). Elisha extrapolates beyond the data. No, No, No. No time to accept. No time to accept, because it was all free from Yahweh. No bargain, no bribe, no great gift. Gehazi the servant has completely misunderstood his master, because he imagines by hook or by crook to be somehow entitled to a return on an Israelite miracle. He imagines that the practice of faith ought to lead to profit.

"Therefore," says the prophet, "the leprosy of Naaman shall cling to you, and to your descendants forever." So he left his presence leprous, as white as snow (v. 27).[8]

His mistake turns out to be a costly misunderstanding. This is, in its completed form, a narrative of complete inversion:

the last first, the first last;

the humbled exalted, the exalted humbled;

the one who loses his life gains, the one who gains loses.

The servant is a dreadful, in-house contrast to the alien Syrian general, the wrong one healed, the home body savaged. You can imagine the terrible, threatening skin of Gehazi. Would that he had a little slave girl (*na'arah qatannah*) who could make him like a little boy (*na'ar qaton*), with innocent baby flesh. He, however, has forfeited his good skin and his good life by taking a gift for profit from the power of the gospel. The narrative ends there, sharp and uncompromising, no second chance for the cunning, greedy servant.

Lukan Futures

The story is strong enough on its own that we may linger a long time over its telling. Beyond its own imaginative say, however, the story has daring futures. It generates futures that, for confessing Christians, lead inescapably to Jesus. Jesus' identity, power, and ministry are in part rooted in these old narrative memories that refuse to stay old or past. They surge up with new truth, new energy, and new healing.

The first of two appeals to our narrative that I shall mention in the belated narrative of Jesus is in *Luke 4:27*. As you know, this is the occasion at Nazareth when Jesus riskily quotes the Isaiah text on Jubilee, and with extended risk asserts, "Today this scripture has been fulfilled in your hearing" (v. 21). Jesus then evokes great opposition to his claim and announcement by saying that the good stuff of Jubilee must be done *outside* of Israel, because it cannot happen inside, here in Nazareth. The look outside is given narrative justification by two references, first from 1 Kings 17:8–16, when Elijah ministers to the widow of Zarephath of Sidon, a woman twice outside as foreigner and widow. His second appeal is to our narrative:

> There were also many lepers in Israel in the time of the prophet Elisha, and none of them was cleansed except Naaman the Syrian (Luke 4:27).

Jesus' imagination and self-discernment are funded precisely by these odd prophetic "legends."

Jesus recognizes in that ancient narrative (and in his own reach outside his home folks) that the healing power of God has no boundary according to us or to our kind. The Syrian general who went back home to play his role as a Syrian is accepted as one who has received the "baby flesh" of God's healing. Meanwhile, the insider, Gehazi, receives a fleshly death threat for not discerning the gift. No wonder that Jesus' listeners that day who see Jesus reach outside are filled with murderous rage.

Second and less directly, in *Luke 17:11—19* Jesus is in a northern village, still remote from Jerusalem. Ten lepers approach him. They keep their distance from him because they are socially infected. Except that he is a healing agent that draws the infected to him the way honey draws flies. They come toward him. They petition him: "Jesus, master, have mercy on us." He says, "Go show yourselves to the priests," an equivalency to Elisha's "Go wash in the Jordan seven times." Go do the routine regimen of healing. Abruptly, immediately, "they were made clean." He exudes power, as did his ancient forebear.

Ten are healed, one comes back to thank. Only one, and the one is a Samaritan. The locals do not bother to send a thank-you note. The Samaritan, the one who is supposed to be a crude, unappreciative oaf, gives thanks. Jesus is dazzled by the unexpected inversion of responses:

"Was none of them found to return and give praise to God except this foreigner?" (v. 18).

Except this foreigner! To be sure, this is a Samaritan and not a Syrian. The plot, however, is the same. The outsider is pitiful and healed, and ends in praise. The point, so characteristic of Luke, is that the gospel is for those beyond; those inside, cast variously as Gehazi and the nine, discern nothing. I am only surprised that the leprosy did not return to the nine who did not give thanks!

Now I push one step beyond the New Testament toward us. The New Testament usage of the narrative suggests a porous, complex interaction of insiders and outsiders in which nothing and nobody stays nicely slotted. Indeed, Gehazi is a cipher for the refusal of "otherness," who thinks that others ought to be exploited. The church, now the one who remembers, treasures, and enacts this narrative, is now in a strange, new place with the demise of old, established powers of Christendom. Everything strange, everything odd, everything alien, everything other, indeed, to parallel Barth, everything *ganz anders*. In our situation, we may ask about this text as an exercise of fidelity in an alien society. I should suggest that in order to grasp our own alienness in faith, we test out each character as alien in the story, that is, not belonging, but engaged in the issue of faith nonetheless. I suggest that in hearing this narrative, we play all roles and consider in each, belonging and not belonging, and being faithful.

1. *The Israelite king* in Samaria, Jehoram. I will not linger over him long. He is ensconced in Samaria. He is the number one "belonger" in the narrative, who evidences no alien quality, no openness to others, no understanding of what is about to happen in the narrative. The narrative is not interested in him, and he is quickly an irrelevance to the plot. He misunderstands everything, and can view the other who comes to him in need only as a ploy or a threat, but not a fellow traveler in need. His single response to the crisis is completely inept and inappropriate (2 Kings 5:7). He does not understand the story in which he is implicated, and so he promptly falls out of the story.

2. *Gehazi* is the other insider who ups the stakes beyond the way of the undiscerning king. Gehazi is deeply Israelite, lives close to the prophet, has a chance to be caught up in the odd ways of the prophet, but he refuses. Perhaps he has spent too much time away from the prophet, for we are told in 8:4, "Now the king was talking with Gehazi, the servant of the man of God." Is that how he spent his afternoons off, in chat time with the king who understood nothing?

So deeply does Gehazi misunderstand that he believes a miracle from the God of Israel is a chance to make a buck. When God's grace is seen as property and not as surprise, as utility and not as sacrament, it becomes an occasion for use. When the gospel is not "made strange," there is a deep chance of "ease in Zion," of thinking, "Now we know it and will administer it for our enhancement." That stance is intolerable, and the outcome is predictable. The leprosy lifted from the Syrian is floating around, looking for a suitable habitat. It lights on Gehazi. The treacherous insider is, by social disease, made an unacceptable outsider. As aliens may enact fidelity, so lack of strangeness is an overture to exploitative infidelity.

3. *Elisha* dominates this narrative, even though he speaks to the general only three quick times (vv. 10, 16, 19) and briefly to Gehazi (vv. 25–26). The prophet is an Israelite, son of Shaphat, whom Elijah recruits (1 Kings 19:19–21). The prophet belongs; except that he belongs not at all. He is outside everything, indeed he is outside time. Scholars have observed that the royal formula ending the reign of Ahaziah (2 Kings 1:17–18) and the opening formula of Jehoram (3:1–3) place the call narrative of Elisha between royal periods, outside the time line of the kings. He does not belong. He is alien. Indeed, we have so many stories about him precisely because Israel cannot decode his strange identity and presence and his odd power. He is indeed other.

He is, moreover, deeply, threateningly faithful to Yahweh. He is the one who enacts Yahweh in a variety of hopeless situations. His fidelity to Yahweh is a refusal to accept any deathly status quo, each time summoning the Easter power of Yahweh into play. He makes that summons in the face of death with the woman's son (chap. 4). He does it economically for the same woman who has lost her turf (8:16). He does it internationally for the Syrian general, for he knows that Yahweh's power for newness is everywhere pertinent and powerful, everywhere waiting to be enacted in the face of the most resistant powers of death, poverty, and leprosy.

4. *The Syrian general* is, on the face of it, an outsider, as Jesus recognizes in Luke 4. Naaman does not belong. Indeed, he is inept when he comes to Israel, not understanding the strange Israelite power arrangements of Yahweh. Like the three wise men, he goes to the king, the last place to find the power for life. He knows he is an outsider, because he brings gifts…bribes. More than that, he wants two mule-loads of Israelite soil, a little of his new home. We are not told if he got them. Perhaps. What interests us, however, is that he knows in his last appeal to the prophet that when he goes home to Syria, it will not any longer be his home. When he worships the Syrian god, it will not be his God. He is not really a Syrian any longer. But he will never be an Israelite. The gift of Yahweh problematizes his existence, so that he is odd and alien wherever he is, and nowhere is ever his home again. He is alien, but he situates his life in a public act of doxology, a deep act of fidelity, for him a dangerous, scandalous act. His displacement permits his doxology; his not belonging lets him announce his new identity.

5. *The nameless young girl* is surely an outsider in Syria, where she lives. She is not acknowledged, not valued, and not free to go home. She is, in my judgment, the pivot of the narrative. She knows who she is; in her displacement she has not forgotten anything. And so in the crisis of leprosy, she gives a bold account of healing, a genuine evangelist. She is not mentioned again, but she makes the entire narrative of new life possible for her "betters." In her witness, she gives strength; in her faith, she preempts Syrian territory for the God of Israel and the prophet in Israel. She does so in deep vulnerability. As a long-term consequence of her telling, the God of Israel is fully thanked by the Syrian general; she, by contrast, is not thanked at all.

Humming Alien Doxologies

This narrative yields no simple slotting of outsider-insider, no settled formula of fidelity or infidelity. The narrative rather presents a cast of characters—so much like us—in a state of liminality, old identities now inadequate, new identities not yet established, all at risk, some characters quite closed, some more open, some blessed and grateful, some frightened, some cursed and silent. We read and are invited to new vistas of identity, new risks, and new doxologies. The characters themselves stay alive through our telling, not settled, because the unsettling issues of life and death are seen to be alive and operative for all who act in this story and all who tell it and all who hear it. All characters wait for the prophetic "go in peace" (5:19). Our life continues to be in the ambiguity of aliens, but braced by an unrestrained, uncompromised doxology. The young girl will probably hum along.

4

The Good News of Bread

2 Kings 6:24—7:20

D. T. Niles, celebrated Sri Lankan ecumenist, has remarked that Christian evangelism is the action of one beggar who has found bread telling other beggars where they also may find bread.[1] It is a similar juxtaposition of *gospel* and *bread* that marks the entry point for the Elisha narrative of 2 Kings 6:24—7:20. Like every practitioner of the good news of the God of Israel, Elisha is in the bread business. Already in 2 Kings 4:42–44, he has taken twenty loaves of barley and fresh ears of grain and has fed a hundred people. In an exchange that is surely echoed in the gospel narrative, his servant resists the idea of feeding so many with so little: "How can I set this before a hundred people?" (see Mk. 8:4). The narrative concludes, after the prophetic act of feeding, "He set it before them, they ate, and had some left, according to the word of the LORD" (v. 44). There was more than enough, because the prophet is an embodiment of the abundance of the creator God! (See Mk. 6:30–44; 8:1–10, both narratives concluding with abundant leftovers, on which see also Mk. 8:19–20.)

Hunger and the Neglected Woman

When we arrive at our narrative in 2 Kings 6:24–25, however, the bread business has come on hard times. Nobody is effective in supplying bread. War has broken out, yet again, between Israel and Syria, just one verse after Elisha had made a great feast that had turned hostility between Israel and Syria to at least a truce (v. 23). But now war again, and with war, a shortage of bread. The juxtaposition of verse 23 and verse 24 suggests an immense connection between *war* and *bread;* where there is war = no bread, where there is bread = no war. The stratagem of Syria, here characteristically presented as the aggressor, is to lay siege to the Israelite capital city of Samaria, to surround the city with troops, cut off supplies, and so starve the city to death. The famine is not a natural disaster but is an intended function and by-product derived from human hostility.

When bread is in short supply, moreover, the price of other food escalates. What food is still available becomes all the more valuable. Even poor food is expensive. The narrator offers two unbelievable examples of the high cost of food. The head of a donkey (perhaps not unlike what we used to call "head-cheese") costs eighty shekels of silver; a small portion of bird manure, dove's dung, costs five shekels. Imagine laying out such cash for this sort of food! The narrative intends us to see the depth of the food crisis. It is legitimate, moreover, to ask who had eighty shekels for food, or even five. Certainly not the poor, the ones who might have regularly relied upon dove dung. The social crisis drives the monied to take the food conventionally left for the poor, leaving the poor, of course, with nothing. The crisis is one of hunger produced by brutal power and the posturing of ambitious military regimes, a crisis acutely experienced by the marginal.

Given this context of acute social crisis in the bread business, the narrative now moves through five scenes, each preoccupied with food (6:26–31; 6:32—7:2; 7:3–10, 11–16, 17–20). The narrative is straightforward about the crisis. There is nothing obscure about the famine, its causes, or its consequences. At the same time, however, the narrative recognizes that there is something odd and inscrutable about the bread. Unlike a transparent understanding of the famine, bread requires pondering, for the life is in the bread. And because of the focus upon the oddness of the bread, I suggest that a powerful undercurrent in the story is the deep awareness in Israel that Yahweh, barely visible but certainly operative in this narrative, is the creator God whose purpose it is that the earth should teem with bread for all. But how can the will of Yahweh for teeming bread emerge in the face of the brute fact of famine? The question haunts the narrative.

The escalating price of food hits the poor first and most acutely. In our first scene (6:26–31), the first voice we hear is that of a woman. The king is mentioned first, but he does not speak. She cries out to the king. She is shrill and insistent. Her voice is the sound of the most needy, most vulnerable, and least expectant. She has no formal access to the king, who is walking on the wall inspecting the military installations, concerned with the threat of the siege (see Isa. 7:3; 36:2). The king is preoccupied with "security matters" and has given no attention at all to the price of bread or to the welfare of the poor. As the nameless woman cries out, she creates a dramatic encounter between power and need, between "security" and "welfare."

She has no right to speak. Except that the desperately hungry do not wait for a right to speak. She will not wait for royal protocol. The one who is most hungry voices her desperate stomach to the one who presides over the food monopoly. If anyone has food it is the king. She speaks abruptly and directly, addressing the king with an imperative: "Save me." She speaks, as Larry Lyke has observed, according to a rhetorical convention whereby the most unprotected (the woman) bids to the official protector.[2] She echoes her sister who had appealed to king David in 2 Samuel 14:4. The king is the only one who stands between her and starvation. But the king, characteristically, is unresponsive. He promptly resists her imperative: "How can I save?" He does not know how to respond to her. He refuses her request by a reference to the proximate sources of food— threshing floor and wine press, grain and wine—that are in a sorry, failed state. These conventional vehicles of food are in any case all shut down. The king calls her attention to his own lack of resources. He has nothing with which to save. But then he abdicates his royal duty and his political-economic responsibility for food management and turns theologian. He prefers to imagine, in his appeal to piety, that "save" means some non-bodily well-being, something other than food, perhaps something more spiritual. He gives a useless theological answer to an economic emergency: "Let Yahweh save you." Yahweh is in the *saving* business, he thinks, but kings are in the *security* business. He is as abrupt and dismissive as she has been abrupt and demanding.

After this initial abrupt royal refusal, the king does trouble to inquire about her need (v. 28). But he asks only after he has refused. Both parties already know that the immediate need is food. The king already knows that and does not need to ask. But the woman's plight is more complicated, a complication designed to underscore the general emergency of the famine. The woman has been tricked by another desperate woman. She colluded with the other woman to share her son as food with the other woman, with the agreement that the second day the son of the other woman would be shared and eaten by the two women. Together they seized the "first day's ration." "We cooked my son and ate him." But then the second woman reneged and saved her own son by hiding him. The presenting problem to the king is that the second woman has reneged on a deal. But the real issue is the wretchedness that has driven them to cannibalism. The mother no longer mothers her son, but now regards him only as food. The dire emergency seems to echo the dire anticipation of Moses:

> In the desperate straits to which the enemy siege reduces you, you will eat the fruit of your womb, the flesh of your own sons and daughters whom the LORD your God has given you. Even the most refined and gentle of men among you will begrudge food to his own brother, to the wife whom he embraces, and to the last of his remaining children, giving to none of them any of the flesh of his children whom he is eating, because nothing else remains to him, in the desperate straits to which the enemy siege will reduce you in all your towns. She who is the most refined and gentle among you, so gentle and refined that she does not venture to set the sole of her foot on the ground, will begrudge food to the husband whom she embraces, to her own son, and to her own daughter, begrudging even the afterbirth that comes out from between her thighs, and the children that she bears, because she is eating them in secret for lack of anything else, in the desperate straits to which the enemy siege will reduce you in your towns. (Deut. 28:53–57)

Moses knows that when people are desperate enough, the thin facade of civility will fail; even the best are reduced to desperate, ignoble measures. To be sure, nothing is said in our narrative of guilt and curse, the context of Moses' anticipation in Deuteronomy 28. The focus rather is on the crisis and not its cause. Any knowing reader, however, understands that the situation is one of curse. Without being explicit, Yahweh is thereby implicated in the food emergency.

The woman wants food. She has made her "supreme sacrifice" of her son and is still desperate. She has eaten her son and her destitution is unrelieved. But the king cannot help. He can grieve. He can acknowledge the degradation of his realm. He can exhibit his sackcloth, his ritual recognition that he presides over a body of death (v. 30). But he is resourceless, helpless, exposed to the desperate woman in his own desperation. When the king is without resources for his needy subject, he is in fact no king at all.

The king's response to the terrible report of the woman is quite unexpected, surely a non sequitur:

> So may God do to me, and more, if the head of Elisha son of Shaphat stays on his shoulders today (v. 31).

How odd! The woman wants food and the king threatens the prophet who has been completely absent from this narrative. It is as though the king is obsessed with the prophet. He knows the name and identity of the prophet. It is as though the king credits the famine to the prophet, even though we have been told that the famine is a function of war, perhaps a measure of the king's failed diplomacy toward Syria. Or perhaps the king understands everything correctly. He knows that the prophet presides over the future of Israel, over the well-being of his realm, over the bread business. He knows about covenant theology, and the curses of Deuteronomy 28. And he knows that the prophets enact the curses of the Torah. In his hostile resolve toward the prophet, the king tacitly admits to the woman that he is resourceless, powerless, without initiative, credibility, or any claim to power. He is as pitiful as is she. Very likely he is not hungry, for he, if anyone, could supply the silver needed for dove's dung. He is, however, as short on authority as she is short on bread. The scene ends binding the pitiful woman and the equally pitiful king in a common despair. The king seems to think the way to solve the food problem is to kill the prophet and so void the curse. He vows to kill the prophet.

But now the scene shifts. We hear no more of the woman. She is immediately forgotten, one more neglected welfare case in a regime that invests all its energy in security. She has performed her harsh function in the narrative. She is to enact and embody, in her grotesque strategy, the depth of the food emergency. She does her narrative work well, for now we know that the food chain that runs from Yahweh to defenseless women has been decisively interrupted, perhaps by covenant curse, more likely by the "fun and games" of war played by the men who never take into full account the women. At the end of the narrative, some will receive food; but not she!

King and Prophet in Theological Dialogue

Now the narrative turns. The woman exits. In this second scene (6:32—7:2), the interface is not needy woman and pitiful king.[3] Now it is desperate king and buoyant prophet. The royal threat against the prophet has been uttered in the last scene, in verse 31, even before the prophet is on the horizon of the narrative. But in this scene, Elisha already knows. He is aware, we know not how, that the king has placed a price on his head. He reminds his cohorts that the king will want to kill him, and he bids them protect him; he is a practical man.

The king's man approaches his house, apparently to kill him. The king is on the heels of his messenger-killer. Perhaps the threat of the king against the prophet, voiced to the woman, was merely rhetoric. Because when the king arrives at the house of the prophet, he does not kill him. He wants to talk; he wants to bluster. He wants to argue. Indeed, he wants to argue theology. In verse 27, we have seen the king's pious response to the woman, "Let Yahweh save you." But now, given the cannibal-evoking depth of the famine, the king no longer expects food from Yahweh for either the woman or for the realm. Thus, he blames Elisha in verse 31; but in verse 33, he knows that the real problem is not Elisha but the God of Elisha. In 1 Kings 18:17, King Ahab had called Elijah "you troubler of Israel." Now in verse 33, this king, son of Ahab, says of Elisha, adopted son of Elijah, "This trouble (*raʿ*) is from Yahweh the LORD."[4] Both Ahab and now his son blame the prophet. Both the king and the king's son recognize that there is trouble in the royal realm beyond their control. Both tacitly recognize that they are indeed not masters in their own house. They cannot quite determine if they should appeal to Yahweh or if they should kill the prophet of Yahweh.

In any case, in the middle of the bread story, we have a theological conversation between king and prophet, two exchanges of royal authority and prophetic response.

Exchange #1: The king asks defiantly, or perhaps with pathos, why should I hope in Yahweh any longer? (v. 33). Perhaps he is asking for reassurance; perhaps this is a royal declaration of unfaith. Either way, it is astonishing that this is the only use of the term "hope" (*yhl*) in all the books of kings. This usage, moreover, is on the lips of the king; the king asks about hope, but then lines out a negation of hope. The king is not a hoper. He has all the data to support his conclusion. There is no bread. Yahweh has not given bread, and there is no reason to expect that Yahweh will give bread any time soon.

The prophetic response: Now speaks Elisha, the one under royal death threat who here, as regularly, contradicts observable reality. The prophet speaks an enigmatic oracle: soon food prices will tumble. Food prices so high as to starve the woman will fall dramatically, because there will be ample food. By tomorrow, a measure of choice meal will sell for a shekel, two measures of barley for a shekel, at the city market. How cheap will be a donkey's head or dove dung, cheap enough for the woman. Bread will be given! But no explanation of how! Prophets do not traffic in explanations.

Exchange #2: Now speaks the king's close advisor upon whom the king relies: "Oh sure! No doubt!" The contempt of disbelief in the prophetic assurance is thick. The anticipation of the prophet will never happen. This high bureaucratic official does not believe in miracles, because he knows about famine. But for purposes of contempt, says he, let's suppose a miracle. Let's suppose there were windows in the sky whereby the great bread resources of heaven were opened and the earth were flooded with bread from heaven. We know there are such supplies of water up there (see Gen. 7:11; 8:3; Job 38:22). But let's suppose instead of rain, already well attested, that there came bread, bread from heaven (as in Ps. 105:40). We all know the manna story, but nobody in the royal environs believes in bread from heaven. Only a pitiful administrator might count on miracles. And even if there were those open windows, there would not be enough bread to lower the price of food. The woman will never afford bread. So the cynical officer speaks the unfaith of the king.

The prophet responds:

You shall see it with your own eyes, but you shall not eat from it (v. 2).

The prophetic word is part assurance, part threat to the royal officer. In scene 2 the reader is placed in a position to decide for the inexplicable assurance of the prophet, who offers no explanation. Or the reader may opt for the cynical realism of the king and his agent, a realism that has only contempt for hope. In the first scene, no bread. In the second scene, bread promised, but also doubted, and certainly not in hand.

Three Options, Three Voices, and the Good News

Now in the third scene, the action shifts abruptly to a very different venue (vv. 3–11). In this scene both king and prophet are absent. The only characters we see are four lepers. These are the lowliest of the low, ranked in repulsion even below the wretched woman of scene one, excluded and degraded, because they are dangerous and contagious, and must be kept out of the places where community life is lived. They are outside the city gate of Samaria. The prophet said that there would be food "at the gate of Samaria" (v. 1). But they are excluded there, even if bread were given.

They may be wretched, excluded, nameless, and despised; but they still want to live. Even the lowly want to live when society is ready to give them up to death—"A living dog is better than a dead lion" (Eccl. 9:4). The lepers consider their desperate plight at the end of the food chain that has run out:

Option A: If we go into Samaria, we will die from famine.

Option B: If we remain outside the city, we will die.

We will die with either option.

Let us consider option C: Let us desert to the Syrians.

They are considering the dreaded Syrians, Israel's durable enemy who lays siege against the city of Samaria. These may be lepers, but they are Israelite lepers. Here are Israelites so desperate that they will take their chance with the enemy, Syria, who is not beset by famine. The lepers act out their desperate plan of desertion to the enemy. They approach the Syrian camp.

Now we are told, as the narrator clues us in, what the lepers themselves do not know (vv. 6–7). The Syrian camp is deserted. The Syrians are gone, having fled. I identified the lepers as the only visible characters in the scene. We will never see the Syrians who have fled. Moreover, we never see Yahweh, who here appears for the only time as an active character. We are told that Yahweh has caused the Syrians to hear—a *hiph'il* form of the verb *shema'*. We do not know how that happened. But trust the causative verb over which Yahweh presides:

Yahweh caused the Syrians to hear,

the voice of chariots,

the voice of horses,

the voice of a great cry.

Three times "voice": *qol, qol, qol.* The voice sounded like an approaching army. It sounded so large and formidable that, according to Syrian intelligence, it could not be a sound made by Israel, because Israel is too small to make such a sound (see Isa. 36:8). There is more here than Israel, Syria has concluded. The Israelites must have summoned as allies the great imperial armies of Egypt and the Hittites, the superpowers of the South and the North. The Syrians imagine that Israel has been able to recruit and mobilize all the military power in the known world…and they flee. They have no alternative, given their reconnaissance on the military situation. The lepers do not know all of that. They only know that the camp is empty, "no one there at all."

But why such a miscalculation on the part of Syria, for Israel had not ventured out of Samaria at all? Well, it was because of Yahweh who, through Elisha, had promised food. Unbeknownst to the desperate woman and beyond the despair of the king, Yahweh was still the hope of Israel, still at work on behalf of Israel. But what a way to work! No explanation is hazarded about the sound. Except that in the great curse recital of Leviticus 26 it is said:

> I will send faintness into their hearts in the lands of their enemies; the sound of a driven leaf shall put them to flight, and they shall flee as one flees from the sword, and they shall fall though no one pursues. They shall stumble over one another, as if to escape a sword, though no one pursues; and you shall have no power to stand against your enemies. (vv. 36–37)

That anticipation is a curse; we are not told that Syria is under curse. But what Yahweh may do to those who earn the wrath of Yahweh (as anticipated in the curse) may also be done to Israel's enemies. Syria is put to flight by anxiety that imagines a crisis. The turn of the narrative is through an imagined scenario that is rooted in anxiety that skews reality. It is all a trick; but it is a trick performed by Yahweh, who, so the narrator does not doubt, stands close behind the action and governs in ways not even the lepers can comprehend.

There is no one there! The lepers draw close to the Syrian camp that is their option C, against the two rejected options of death. The lepers go to the edge of the camp and cautiously enter the first tent. There are no people, no Syrians, no danger. The tent is loaded with goodies, because the Syrians left in a frantic, mistaken hurry. In the tent the lepers eat and drink…all they want. Then they lay hands on silver, gold, and clothing. They take it and hide it. They return and enter another tent, and take and hide what is there. Another and another and another, all the tents, all the silver and gold, all the garments, all the drink, all the bread. Notice well all the bread. These are the last becoming the first. We are watching a transfer of goods, an inversion of history, all wrought in an inscrutable way by a *hiph'il* verb that created a world-changing miscalculation. The narrator does not explain, does not even reflect, but simply tells. We watch the ones who were to die come to a full, joyous life—"a good measure, pressed down, shaken together, running over" (Luke 6:38). There is, for the four lepers, an abundance, more than enough; loaves abound!

But then the frenzy of abundance is interrupted by a second thought on the part of the lepers. They may be outsiders, even deserters. But they are nonetheless still subjects of the king in Samaria. They owe him yet some loyalty because they have no wish to become Syrians. Or perhaps they are so schooled in the Torah commandments that they know they cannot enjoy in private this immense gift from Yahweh while they do not share with their fellows. Either on pragmatic grounds of fear or on ethical grounds of covenant, they know that a private gorging is irresponsible. It is wrong, and if their find is not reported, they will be found guilty. They must break off their gleeful orgy of confiscation in order to share the find. They must tell the others where the bread is that they have found.

In the midst of their fear of being found out, the lepers make the most remarkable statement one to another:

This is a day of good news…let us go and tell the king's household (v. 9).

They are to be messengers to the king (who characteristically sends messengers and does not receive them, certainly not lepers). They are to tell the king where the food is, the king who is in the bread business but who is all out of resources. Most remarkably, the term "good news" is the word *basarah*, the term used in Isaiah 40:9, 41:27, and 52:7 to mean the "gospel" announcement of Yahweh's victory over Babylon, which will release captive Israel. The term means news or good news, but it is not everywhere "gospel." In some places it is simply "news." The only other use of the term in Kings is in 1 Kings 1:42, where Adonijah expects the good news of kingship that is denied him. This is the only other usage, and no one would suggest that here the term means gospel, for it is on the lips of lepers and refers only to a cache of enemy plunder that will break the Israelite famine.

Except I propose precisely that here this word, *basarah*, on the lips of the lepers is exactly the term "gospel," the good news that Yahweh has broken the famine with a supply of food, a supply that fulfills the assurance of the prophet in 7:1. This is indeed the gospel announcement of a beggar who has found bread, going to tell other beggars where they have found food.

I propose that this rather enigmatic and complex narrative turns exactly on the enigma of verse 6 and the responding testimony of verse 9, for gospel always consists in *an enigmatic, inexplicable act of Yahweh* plus *the human voicing* of the turn Yahweh has wrought.[5] The enigma is that *a sound* turned circumstance. The only thing not enigmatic is that Yahweh is the singular, unambiguous cause. Yahweh's act is nothing more than sneaking into the Syrian camp and saying, "Boo!" But that is enough. And then, on the part of those who benefit from the turn caused by Yahweh's intervention, there is a compulsion to tell, to let the others in on the good news: "Let us go and tell the king's household." Go and tell!

The world has been turned, just as the prophet said. But we are surely to notice that the prophet is in no way connected by the narrative with the "boo" of Yahweh that changed the world. We have no hint in verse 1 that the prophet knows how the bread will be given, and no suggestion that the prophet instigated or participated in the three-fold "voice." The prophet is a bread man who has promised and is now vindicated. Perhaps the intention of the narrative is to celebrate prophetic authority and reliability.

But if we read carefully and closely, we are bound to notice that the magisterial way whereby Yahweh causes bread (by routing the Syrians) is beyond and beneath any prophetic performance. The bread appears not according to prophetic initiative, but according to the inscrutable, hidden, unacknowledged work of Yahweh that defies comment. While this is a prophetic narrative, the wonder of "gospel bread" is not a function of prophetic intervention but of providential productivity all on its own, without human agency or utterance. The world in its workings produces bread, but Yahweh's bread involves the "fear and dread" in which Yahweh traffics beyond human enactment (see Ex. 15:16; Deut. 2:25, 11:25; Ps. 105:38). It is acceptable for Elisha to assure and promise; in the end, however, this bread is Yahweh's own doing.

The lepers know. And they faithfully report, thus escaping censure for desertion; they fulfill their obligation—unlike Achan in Joshua 7—not to withhold Yahweh's goodness from the community. So they report:

> We went to the Aramean camp, but there was no one to be seen or heard there, nothing but the horses tied, the donkeys tied, and the tents as they were (v. 10).

Surely we may be permitted to notice that while they report on the condition of the camp, they did not report on all they had consumed or stashed away for themselves. Perhaps they judged that the messenger is entitled to a reward for bringing the news. In any case, they appear to have taken care of themselves first.

They are still lepers after they report their find; they will now disappear from the narrative. We do not know what happened to them. The narrative is no longer interested in them. They are dropped as the woman of the first scene is forgotten. Probably they return to their hidden treasures. In any case, they have contributed decisively to the narrative. They have overcome the hopelessness of the king about bread. They have, moreover, enacted the prophetic promise. They are lepers who only approach the city, still not given access. They tell the gatekeeper, only the one at the gate. The word of gospel is relayed, as it always is, relayed by many witnesses, to the seat of power:

> Then the gatekeepers called out and proclaimed it to the king's household (v. 11).

The relay is not unlike the better-known example in Isaiah 52:7–9:

> How beautiful upon the mountains
>   are the feet of the messenger
>   who announces peace,
> who brings good news,
>   who announces salvation,
>   who says to Zion, "Your God reigns."
> Listen! Your sentinels lift up their voices,
>   together they sing for joy;
> for in plain sight they see
>   the return of the LORD to Zion.
> Break forth together into singing
>   you ruins of Jerusalem;
> for the LORD has comforted his people,
>   he has redeemed Jerusalem.

The messengers tell the sentinel. The sentinel tells the king's household, and the city rejoices. The message is the same here as in the better-known case. It is good news from Yahweh. One aspect is bread:

> Ho, everyone who thirsts,
>   come to the waters;
> and you that have no money,
>   come, buy and eat!
> Come, buy wine and milk
>   without money and without price. (Isa. 55:1)

Bread signifies well-being, freedom from oppression, and the end of threat. The lepers that day had "beautiful feet," and their message was welcome. They let the king know, mired in his deep despair, that he was safe and the bread supply was renewed. The gospel carriers stayed outside. All they could do was tell the news. It remained then for the news to be received and accepted as a transformative consequence concerning those who heard.

According to the Word of the Lord

All that remains is for the king and his household to receive and accept the news of bread, and to act on it. The king, however, being the king, makes the reception of the good news a great deal more complex than it need be (vv. 12–16). The lepers can only report what they know; they do not know what the narrator has told us about Yahweh and the causative verb. All the lepers know, and therefore all they can report, is that the Syrian camp is deserted. The lepers, so pleased with their find, do not speculate or offer any reason for such an odd discovery. Perhaps a wiser, more trusting interpreter of the Syrian camp could have thought Yahwistically and would have said, "Well of course, Yahweh has frightened the Syrians and they have fled because the dread of Yahweh has come upon them." But such an interpretation would have required, beyond faith, prescience about the narrative and its decisive verb. The king, awakened in the night by the gatekeepers, is not capable of such theological discernment. Awakened in the middle of the night, the king falls back on his first instinct. After all, he is an Omride, a son of Ahab, a royal outfit not known for Yahwistic acumen. We have seen, moreover, that he has abandoned all hope in Yahweh; he is fated to receive the gospel word according to his defining despair, sure to misconstrue.

The king is prepared to believe only the worst, a worst that makes no reference to Yahweh and that entertains no good news. Half asleep, he makes a judgment that will determine policy: "It's a trick!" Since there is no Yahweh on his screen, there are only Syrians. And since there are only Syrians, they must have initiated this ruse in order to entrap Israel. The lepers have data but offer no explanation. The king, conversely, has no data but offers an explanation, fueled by his great fear and his equally great despair: "It is a trap and when we go out of Samaria to their camp, they will capture us and take the city. It's a strategy for ending the famine-producing siege of Samaria." There is no basis in any data for this judgment by the king, except that the king is fearful. We have already seen that the Syrians in verse 6 acted in fear and fled before an imaginary Israel. And now, in complementary fashion, Israel acts in fear and reacts to an imaginary Syria. Again, so it seems, the power of fear and anxiety are defining for communities that have excluded Yahweh from the equation:

> I will send faintness into their hearts in the lands of their enemies; the sound of a driven leaf shall put them to flight, and they shall flee as one flees from the sword and they shall fall though no one pursues. They shall stumble over one

another, as if to escape a sword, though no one pursues. (Lev. 26:36–37)

The narrator creates an odd scene in which the two states—Israel and Syria—are both driven by fear, both forming policy and taking actions premised on a mirage of threat. Both thereby engage in actions that are against their best interest, because neither Israel nor Syria is able to reckon with Yahweh, the decisive but unnoticed force and agent in the narrative. (I might observe in passing that it was "the "Communist threat" that for a very long time managed U.S. foreign policy, a threat in some great measure imagined and continued as imagined threat in the Vietnam war.)

Fortunately, the king not only has sensible advisors, but he heeds them (vv. 13–15). The advisors propose to the king that a reconnaissance party gather more data, so that a mistaken response is not made on unbased imagination. The proposal is five spies on five horses; they send two. We are not told why only two are sent of the five proposed, but it is apparently an act of caution. The spies go all the way to the Jordan seeking the Syrian army that is allegedly lying in wait. They never, so far as we are told, find the army of Syria; but they go far enough to see that the siege of Samaria has been lifted. There are no Syrians left as a threat to the city.

But the absence of Syrians is only a negative part of what the scouts find. They also report the residue of Syrian panic. The landscape all the way from the city to the river is strewn with Syrian property "the whole way." The retreating, frightened Syrian army dropped garments and equipment all the way as it fled. Partly they were in a hurry and carelessly dropped things. Partly they dropped things in order to travel light and go faster. The scene is one of an army in humiliating disarray. The king, like the lepers, has no idea that this panic and disarray are a response to the sounds made by Yahweh, who conjured threat where there was none. It is Yahweh who has routed Syria. It is Yahweh who has delivered Samaria. It is Yahweh who has given food. It is Yahweh who has given life and possibility back to this hapless Omride king. It is all Yahweh, but nobody in the narrative knows it. Nobody knows except us hearers. We are the ones who connect the "good news" of bread with the God who has worked that good news, the God who, except for us readers, remains completely incognito in the story.

When finally and fully known, the news in the city is that Syria is gone. It is uncommonly good news. The Israelites, after the manner of the lepers, confiscate the rich supplies of the Syrian camp (v. 16). The scene is one of desperately hungry people swarming over the enemy camp, perhaps gloating, but mostly grabbing and not having time to gloat. The scene is not unlike the peasants rushing the Marcos palace in Manila: partly need, partly greed, partly anger, a violent seizure by those so long denied and disadvantaged. They found a great deal in the Syrian camp, "far more abundantly" than the lepers had wanted or could imagine. As a consequence, the market had a run on food, so much food that the famine-driven costs of food in 6:25 collapsed and returned to normal. By the time the new food supplies—made possible by the sounds of Yahweh—had come into the city, the prices had plummeted and were again reasonable:

> So a measure of choice meal was sold for a shekel, and two measures of barley for a shekel (v. 16).

Bread could again be purchased by poor people.

This phrasing of prices is familiar to us. This is exactly what the prophet had anticipated in verse 1. It all happened "according to the word of the Lord," the word that frightened Syria, and that redressed food supplies, the word carried by the prophet. It turns out that neither the Israelite king nor the Syrian army mattered at all. It all happened inscrutably. The prophet may have said more than he knew; he gave no hint of "the sound" of Yahweh that would change everything. In the end, what he said was reliable, because he knew of another governance that neither the pitiful Israelite king nor the panicked Syrian army had taken into account.

The One Who Sees but Does Not Eat

The narrative likely should end in verse 16 with the climactic phrase "according to the word of the Lord." The narrator, however, has some unfinished business. The final scene is a narrative reprise on the initial prophetic exchange of verses 1–2 (vv. 17–20). We have been told of the people's surge to the Syrian food supplies. That report, however, has been generic. Now, in this final statement, the report is quite specific and refers to only one man, the king's captain we have encountered in verse 12. He had the high office and responsibility "in charge of the gate." He determined who had access to the royal center. Access was all controlled and administered and paced in order to maintain a civil procedure.

Hungry hordes, however, do not slow for civil procedure and do not respect bureaucratic protocol, even when it is royal. They rushed to the food; in doing so, they trampled the king's officer. The verb is one of violence, often used for horses walking over humans (as in 9:33). Here there are no horses, only an endless stream of eager, irrepressible human folk who will not be detained by royal officials who always want to administer the food. The narrator fudges slightly, for it is said that this is "just as the man of God had said." In fact Elisha had not anticipated a trampling but had only said, "You will see but not eat."

The point nonetheless is close enough that the narrator can appeal to and quote the ominous exchange of verses 1–2, so that we do not miss the point.

The prophet had said:

Two measures of barley shall be sold for a shekel, and a measure of choice meal for a shekel, about this time tomorrow in the gate of Samaria (v. 18; see v. 1).

The captain had replied in cynical disbelief:

"Even if the LORD were to make windows in the sky, could such a thing happen?" (v. 19; see v. 2).

The prophet had defiantly answered the captain:

You shall see it with your own eyes, but you shall not eat from it (v. 19; see v. 2).

The narrator delights to reiterate the entire conversation as a point of vindication. And then the narrative, returning to verse 17, adds the final verdict on the captain that fully certifies the prophet: It did indeed happen to him; the people trampled him to death in the gate (v. 20).

Literally, "It was so to him." He was trampled. He had seen the food. But he did not eat it. He had situated his life in royal skepticism, bound to his king, who now had abandoned him. The bread never reached him in time. He died at his post, maintaining order, skeptical, without hope, trampled. He was never convinced in time that the prophet, who characteristically violates the data at hand, is closer to the reality of lived life than is all royal management.

Hidden Providence and Expressed Gospel

As usual, the narrator does not interpret or give us the meaning of such an enigmatic tale. That is all left to us. The narrative is complicated, not simple or direct. We may suggest the following as listening pointers:

1. The narrative is clearly concerned, as are all this cluster of stories, with the tense *interface of king and prophet,* legitimated royal authority and the ominous alternative of the prophet who lives at a distance from official power. As is usual, moreover, the prophet is shown to have the authority for life that the king does not at all possess. The king abandons hope in God's future (6:33). His captain, moreover, is completely resistant to the prophetic assurance (7:2). The prophet prevails, and the captain, in lieu of the king, suffers the fatal consequence of resistance.

It is odd, however, that the prophet-king (including the king's captain) encounter is in fact situated in only a few verses of the long narrative; there is the initial encounter in 6:32—7:2 and the confirming reprise in 7:17–20. That is all. In fact, the contest of power and authority that occupies this prophetic narrative is, for the most part, marginal and does not dominate the narrative. For that reason we may look to a second, different accent.

2. In the central part of the narrative (7:3–16), the king is not really a player, except the notice in 7:12 that he completely misperceives what is happening. He is an irrelevance to the strange turn by which his hungry people become an exultant, fed people. And for that matter, the prophet is nowhere to be seen in these verses, nor did the prophet in fact anticipate the turn in the form it took. In these central verses, *the primal actor*—acting only once but decisively—is Yahweh. It is Yahweh who "causes to hear." Everything depends upon that moment: (a) the deception of the Syrians, (b) the discovery of the lepers, and (c) the emancipation of the people of Samaria. This is a Yahweh-wrought wonder that depends upon no human agent and is linked to the prophet only loosely. When Yahweh's work is so direct but hidden and beyond human discernment, we are in the realm of Yahweh's providential activity, the management of creation for the care and preservation of Yahweh's people in the world. I accent this point because it is likely to be missed in our preoccupation with "prophet

versus king." The narrative pivots on the recognition that turns happen in the affairs of human society that have no proximate cause, no human agent, but are indeed the mysterious working of Yahweh in ways that not even the prophet can specify. There are holy forces at work beyond human intentionality.

3. There is only one modest, but crucial addendum to the free working of Yahweh's hidden providential rescue. The role of the lepers is decisive. We may notice who they are and what they do. Their identity, as they remain nameless and undifferentiated, is never given. They are the lowest of the lowly, always destitute and around the edges of society. They have, moreover, no noble or pious purpose. They aim, as best they can, to stay alive, even if they must behave as deserters and therefore traitors. Conventional loyalties are a luxury they cannot afford.

There is a remarkable mismatch between their (lack of) identity and their crucial function in the narrative. The lepers are the ones who trigger the turn of the narrative in Samaria from death to life. Everything depends upon their testimony as they tell of their "gospel day," their day of good news. I have elsewhere observed that the *happening* of good news does not effectively count until it is *told* as good news.[6] The deserted Syrian camp could have lain there deserted and dormant forever, had the lepers not told. The wondrous supplies of food could have been available near at hand while the city of Samaria mistakenly starved under the imagined siege, unless the lepers had told the news that Yahweh had penetrated the Syrian camp to make all things new. Thus *the hiddenness of divine providence*—with Yahweh's resolve to preserve, defend, and care for Israel—depends upon *the announcement that makes available*. If the first beggar does not tell where the food is, the second beggar will never eat. Thus the strange juxtaposition of *hidden providence* and *expressed gospel*, the first the work of Yahweh, the second the work of nameless beggars, together power this story of food:

> But how are they to call on one in whom they have not believed? And how are they to believe in one of whom they have never heard? And how are they to hear without someone to proclaim him? And how are they to proclaim him unless they are sent? As it is written: "How beautiful are the feet of those who bring good news." (Rom. 10:14–15)

The lowliest evangelist is recruited in the service of the inscrutable power of providence.

4. The themes of *prophet-king* and *providence-testimony* are facets of *the bread story*. This story is a meditation upon the gift of bread in a disordered world. The problem of the narrative is famine produced by siege, human hunger evoked by human violence. The narrative never says so, but I have cited two evidences that the power of curse is operative here, curse stated in the old traditions that expose the consequences of human violence:

The curse of hunger:

> In the desperate straits to which the enemy siege reduces you, you will eat the fruit of your womb, the flesh of your own sons and daughters whom the LORD your God has given you (Deut. 28:53).

The curse of inordinate fear:

> The sound of a driven leaf shall put them to flight, and they shall flee as one flees from the sword, and they shall fall though no one pursues (Lev. 26:36).

Both hunger and fear are abnormal in a world properly governed by Yahweh. The narrative is propelled by the awareness that royal policy has made everything abnormal, distorted, and dysfunctional. Thus we begin with the wonder: Can the curse be lifted? Can the hunger be overcome? Can the fear be assuaged?

The narrative drives toward bread; every scene asks about bread.

Scene 1 (6:24–31): The woman has no bread and the king cannot produce it.

Scene 2 (6:32—7:2): The prophet promises bread and diminished food prices, but the royal captain cannot believe.

Scene 3 (7:3–10): The lepers find bread, made available by Yahweh's sounds; they tell the royal household of bread found.

Scene 4 (7:11–16): Overriding royal misperception, the people of Samaria escape the besieged city and find bread in the field, in the Syrian camp, bread left by Syria, bread released by the sound of Yahweh, bread reported by the lepers.

Scene 5 (7:17–20): The bread is given as promised, but the captain refuses and dies in a trampling, unable to believe that bread will be given beyond failed royal strategies.

Yes, of course, "Man does not live by bread alone." But neither man nor woman will live without bread. And so all the powers of Yahweh are here mobilized to bring bread amidst famine, to bring blessing amidst curse, to give life amidst death. This is a narrative of the bread of life, given providentially, told by the least qualified of evangelists.

The final astonishment is that the bread can well up where it is not expected. It can well up here, because the creator who "gives seed to the sower and bread to the eater" (Isa. 55:10) will not quit until all are fed. So Israel confesses in its doxologies:

> These all look to you
> to give them their food in due season;
> when you give to them, they gather it up;
> when you open your hand, they are filled with good
> things (Ps. 104:27–28).

> The eye of all look to you,
> and you give them their food in due season.
> You open your hand
> satisfying the desire of every living thing (Ps. 145:14–15).

The captain, in his resistance, had nonetheless hinted at the wonder of Yahweh's capacity to feed:

> Even if the LORD were to make windows in the sky, could such a thing happen? (v. 2).

In his very denial, the king's agent asks a question that remains unanswered. He affirms that Yahweh has bread beyond royal administration. The captain does not intend it, but we may take his sweeping affirmation-in-denial to be an allusion to the "bread of heaven" in Exodus 16. This is bread beyond merit or explanation. One would not, at first glance, link manna and the plundered bread of the Syrians; but they are of a piece, enigmatic, unexpected, given by Yahweh.

In the Christian tradition, we extrapolate this wondrous capacity of the creator who cares for and protects. This footnote to the manna narrative, in Christian tradition, turns up in the wonders of Jesus. In Mark's review session, Jesus instructs his disciples by a series of questions that are at the same time affirmations and rebukes:

> "Why are you talking about having no bread? Do you still not perceive or understand? Are your hearts hardened? Do you have eyes, and fail to see? Do you have ears, and fail to hear? And do you not remember? When I broke the five loaves for the five thousand, how many baskets full of broken pieces did you collect?" They said to him, "Twelve." "And the seven for the four thousand, how many baskets full of broken pieces did you collect?" And they said to him, "Seven." (Mk. 8:17–20)

And then in a final impatience, Jesus adds, "Do you not yet understand?" Understand about bread, about gift, about providence, about the working of creation in abundance beyond administration, about the full embodiment of Yahweh's bread-giving capacity in Jesus of Nazareth. From our narrator toward the gospel accounts, everything turns on unexpected, inexplicable bread.

And Never Be Hungry Again

Now I understand that I have taken great liberties in moving this little story backward toward manna and forward toward Jesus. Some will say that the story does not carry all of that freight, or that it has little explicit theological intentionality. Moreover, all the bread that is given in the story is what can be taken from the enemy in a ruse. This is no new bread, no bread Yahweh has baked afresh, but only usurpation of bread in keeping with the kinds of usurpations of bread that hostile people do with their neighbors. The story is at most a trace: a quixotic, playful trace of surprise, not high theology, not great assurance, not miracle.

But of course, that is how the hidden gospel of lepers—of nobodies—works, not grand claim, but a tale told, a surprise reported, an oddity celebrated; of such fragile data is the evangel constituted. The claim for Jesus in the Fourth Gospel is more sweeping and more elegant:

> I am the bread of life. Your ancestors ate the manna in the wilderness, and they died. This is the bread that comes down from heaven, so that one may eat of it and not die. I am the

living bread that came down from heaven. Whoever eats of
this bread will live forever; and the bread that I will give for
the life of the world is my flesh. (Jn. 6:48–51)

This bread, in its primal claim, is not very different from our
narrative. These are memories told, "so that you may come to believe"
(Jn. 20:31). Our narrative is an early telling, by early evangelists, "that
you may come to believe," believe there is bread. That telling by
nameless lepers turned the world at the time. Every time a beggar tells
where there is bread, another beggar may eat. As the beggars tell and
eat and share, it is in hope that "they will never be hungry" (Jn. 6:35).

5

Tell Me All the Great Things

2 Kings 8:1–6

The ministry of Elisha is profoundly pastoral and threateningly public. His work is characteristically addressed simultaneously both to personal care and to public transformation. The twinning of these aspects of his work in the narrative memory of Israel is due, no doubt, to the deep conviction of the narrative that Yahweh's intention, for which Elisha is a primal carrier, is always concerned for every facet of life, both personal and public. And therefore any faith rooted in the memory of Elisha must take care at the same time to be pastoral and public. We may see this twinned agenda in this narrative in 2 Kings 8:1–7, which is shaped into four brief scenes.

The Shunammite Woman

In the initial scene of verses 1–2, Elisha is pastorally attentive. He addresses the Shunammite woman who had been his friend and patron in chapter 4. In that narrative, his response to her friendship had been to give her a son and then to raise that same son back to life. Or as this opening verse has it, to "cause him to live." Elisha had enacted the lively power of Yahweh in her life, and now she has every reason to trust him and to heed his counsel in her current dilemma.

His word to her is an imperative rooted in a deep concern for her well-being. His counsel to her connects her life in inescapable ways to the public crisis soon to come. The public crisis soon to come is a famine that will last seven devastating years. She is to flee it, or else she and her restored son will starve to death. The prophet here does not reflect on the coming famine, except to take it as a life-threatening given in the future of Israel. There is to be no safe, private oasis from the famine.

- Famine is the result of drought, and we have seen already in the Elijah narrative that drought is *decreed by Yahweh* as a strategy against the House of Omri, the dynasty that is the peculiar target of the Yahwism of Elijah and Elisha. The drought-producing famine aims to topple delegitimated royal power; except that the threat aimed at the royal house always hits non-royal others first, especially the vulnerable and marginated, like this woman who is here without a man in a patriarchal society.
- The famine, as we see in 2 Kings 6, is a *man-made crisis*, a product of military activity. To be sure, the famine in 2 Kings 6 is local, pertaining to the siege of the capital city of Samaria; this coming crisis is broader, threatening to envelop the entire populace. The connection, however, is close enough to see that it is aggressive, acquisitive human conduct that produces famine.
- The famine is *a breakdown in the food chain*, attesting to the fragility of the fruitful stratagems of creation. The God who "gives seed to the sower and bread to the eater" is either unwilling or unable to sustain the gifts of abundance in certain circumstances (Isa. 55:10).
- It takes no imagination to translate the threat to creation, in biblical thematic, into our own contemporary ecological, *environmental crisis*. Life itself is under siege; daily existence—always fragile—is now even more at risk.

"Famine" is a dread word for a dread threat; it calls into question all conventional conduct and policy, all conventional assumptions and assurances…social, ethical, theological. The initial prophetic utterance here indicates the deep risk that underlies this narrative.

This dread future evokes an imperative from Elisha to the woman: "Rise, go." Leave your settled life, depart your plausibility structure. "Rise, go, sojourn (*ger*)." "Rise, go, sojourn wherever you can sojourn."

The abrupt displacement urged is to leave all that is settled and take on an unsettled, vulnerable, dislocated existence, assuming that wherever you go, you will be marginalized and less than secure. Indeed, the prophet has no suggestion to the woman about the best place to go. He only knows that Israel will become a land of death. She is to become a refugee without a safe place. The triad of imperatives is not an unfamiliar cadence for readers of Israel's text, for it is parallel to the initial imperative of Yahweh to Abraham: Go from your country and your kindred and your father's house (Gen. 12:1).

To be sure, Abraham in Gen. 12:1 is not compelled by famine or dire necessity but only by vocation. By 12:10, however, we read:

Now there was a famine in the land [the new land of promise to which Abraham had gone]. So Abram went down to Egypt to reside there as an alien (*ger*), for the famine was severe in the land.

That episode, moreover, shows Abraham—and more especially Sarah—to be deeply at risk. Lands filled with food tend not to be excessively hospitable toward fugitives from hunger who come there for food. The woman on Elisha's horizon is to replicate the risks of father Abraham. Likely we should not make too much theologically of this parallel, for this same enterprise is endlessly reenacted by the marginal in an at-threat environment where food is scarce. It is here an oddly Israelite move, but it is at the same time a generic human response frequently forced upon the marginal.

The woman obeyed the prophetic imperative immediately. She trusted his word and set out. She went—of all places—to the land of the Philistines! She sojourned (*ger*) there seven years, the duration of the famine. The prophet had not told her where to go; presumably she started out and stopped at the first place where she found food—among the Philistines! They had food—unlike Israel. The famine did not extend to the coastland, perhaps because the land and water were more reliable; or more likely she found food there, in Yahwistic horizon, because Yahweh was not trying to starve out a dynasty among the Philistines as was being attempted in Samaria.

Israelites do not commonly flee to the Philistines. Perhaps the term "Philistine" is not to be taken seriously, for certainly the narrative has no interest in geography. Perhaps the term means nothing more than "other," that is, non-Israelite.[1] In any case, as her departure from the land replicates the originary journey of Abraham, so perhaps her arrival and sojourn in Philistia replicates David, the last Israelite to flee there for sanctuary. Being in Philistia, for a self-conscious Israelite, is no secure thing. Indeed, David laments to Saul concerning his status as "other" in Philistia:

> They have driven me out today from my share in the heritage of the LORD, saying, "Go, serve other gods." Now therefore, do not let my blood fall to the ground, away from the presence of the LORD (1 Sam. 26:18–20).

The woman does not put it as David did. Indeed, she does not put it at all, for she does not speak. She is not so theologically, ideologically alert as the narrator requires David to be. Nonetheless, she is in a strange place, a marginalized alien in pursuit of bread, but at risk about everything else.

The Cry

All of that, however, is simply a setup for the problem of this narrative. The second scene, as I divide it, consists solely in verse 3. The famine is now over. The threat is lifted. The woman can come home. The narrative is noticeably terse. There is nothing celebrative or exultant about her return to Israel. It is all very matter-of-fact. The narrative tells us nothing about her return, how she found things, or what she did…except for one defining thing.

She went to "cry out" to the king. The NRSV translates, she "set out to appeal." The translation shows the interpretive judgment, surely correct, that this "cry" is not the shrieking of a hysterical woman but is the filing of a formal complaint in a legal procedure.[2] The formal complaint is the right of a subject—even a woman subject—to petition the throne to redress a wrong. The juridical rhetoric of Old Testament Israel is everywhere apparent, so this woman is doing what a wronged subject must do. She "cries out" to the king (see 4:1; 6:26).

The rhetoric of cry is taken up in the Old Testament for juridical protest:

> You shall not abuse any widow or orphan. If you do abuse them, when they *cry out* to me, I will surely heed their cry; my wrath will burn, and I will kill you with the sword, and your wives shall become widows and your children orphans.

If you lend money to my people, to the poor among you, you shall not deal with them as a creditor; you shall not exact interest from them...if your neighbor *cries out* to me, I will listen, for I am compassionate (Ex. 22:22–27).

The same cry, moreover, is enacted in the Psalter:

Hear my cry, O God;
> listen to my prayer.
From the end of the earth I call to you,
> when my heart is faint (Psalm 61:1–2).

O LORD, God of my salvation,
> when, at night, I cry out in your presence,
let my prayer come before you;
> incline your ear to my cry (Psalm 88:1–2).

With my voice I cry to the LORD;
> with my voice I make supplication to the LORD.
I pour out my complaint before him;
> I tell my trouble before him...
I cry to you, O LORD;
> I say, "You are my refuge,
> my portion in the land of the living." (Psalm 142:1–2, 5)[3]

Ancient Israel is a litigious society. Yahweh is drawn into the litigation and expected to respond; no less the king as the principal judicial officer is obliged to respond to such complaint, even from the lowly. The woman, with great resolve and determination, insists on recovery and restoration of her property. Forceful, insistent "cry" matters to the redress of wrong, as in Luke 18:1–8.

The petition of the woman to the royal court is for "her house and her field," her property. It was hers, but she has been gone seven years. The neighbors may have been friendly toward her, maybe not. (We have learned of late about Serbs seizing Albanian property and of Albanians seizing Serb property; it is like that in every displacing society.) Entitlement is so flimsy and at risk when the social infrastructure is in jeopardy. Seven years is in any case a long time; seven years of absence is a long time, and encroachment on her property was inevitable. The narrative does not tell us what happened to her house and field. We know from 4:9 that she was a woman of means, enough means to add a room to her house. Perhaps the house and field were taken up in the regularities of commerce and sold off. Perhaps when abandoned they reverted to the throne. In any case, when she got back to her home, her home was gone. She was entitled; but it is gone. And she appeals.

Great Things

The narrative, so to say, moves the camera enough for us to judge that in verses 4–5, we are in a different scene in a different venue. In the new scene, the king is there. We are in the royal chambers with the nameless king, son of Ahab. With him, most remarkably, is Gehazi, servant of Elisha. We are surprised to find him there, because his proper place and function are with Elisha, who has his own dense relationship with the king. We might wonder what Gehazi is doing there, but the narrator does not signal any unease at his presence in the royal domain. Perhaps it is his day off, and he is free to do as he pleases.

What we know of Gehazi, prior to this odd expose, is confined to two narratives. In chapter 4 where the Shunammite woman, our present protagonist, would have known him, he is for the most part a "gofer" for the prophet. In 4:31, however, Gehazi has some illusion of his own importance and authority. At the behest of the prophet himself, he takes the staff of Elisha and tries to heal the dead boy by his handling of the prophetic staff. Because the prophet instructed him to do so, we think he surely will not fail or be faulted for the attempt. Both the prophet and his servant thought for a moment that prophetic healing power could be mobilized by remote control, by the blessed staff in the absence of the prophet. The stratagem does not work, indicating that Gehazi possesses none of the power or authority of the prophet.

The second, less reputable appearance of Gehazi is in chapter 5 concerning the healing of Naaman, the Syrian general. The woman from chapter 4 likely would not have known about the incident in chapter 5. In this narrative, Gehazi is exposed as an unprincipled extortionist. After the healing of the Syrian general, on his own Gehazi tries to exploit the healing by the prophet to raise a little cash for himself on the side. The prophet knows of his initiative, reprimands him, and subjects him to the curse of leprosy. The two episodes together suggest that Gehazi is an ambitious sort and not fully to be trusted. Nothing, however, is made of these matters in our present narrative.

Here Gehazi is chatting up the king. We are not told how he got access to the king, except that this is a small, informal society. Perhaps he is an intimate of the king; perhaps has a special permit for this occasion. Either way, the meeting of the servant and the king is not propelled, so far as we are told, by any agenda or any explicit purpose. The conversation between the two seems easy, natural, and without a focus.

That is, without a focus until the king says to Gehazi, "So, tell me about Elisha your master." More specifically, "Tell me all the great things that Elisha has done" (v. 4). This request for data is the pivot point of the entire narrative. We cannot determine the tone of the king's request:

- It may be an innocent inquiry as the two men gossip about many things, Gehazi's employer included.
- It may be an earnest inquiry—the king has heard rumors, is awed by the prophet and really wants to know. Perhaps the king can be enthusiastic that such wonders take place in his realm, on his watch. In any case, there is no royal animosity to the prophet in this narrative.
- It could be, to the contrary, like Herod in Matthew 2:8, that the king feels threatened by the wonder worker who has seized the initiative from the king and thereby unsettles the realm. In this event, the king wants data to build a case against the one who is subverting the royal authority, as an "enemy" of the king (see 1 Kings 21:20).
- Or it could be that the king is sarcastic: "Tell me about the miracles," and then the two of them have a good chuckle, for both in their cynicism know there is no such thing as a miracle. To be sure, Gehazi has witnessed them, but perhaps in a flat, royal environment, he can be gently pressured to mock and dismiss what he has seen and heard if it violates royal permit.

The question of the king dominates the narrative. If it is in any sense a good-faith question, it is a dazzling moment in the life of Israel. We know about "truth speaking to power." But here it is power asking about truth. And whenever power asks about truth, power is by that much impinged upon and transformed. The question perhaps stands with these other, familiar questions from power to truth.

Zedekiah in secret to Jeremiah:

"Is there any word from the LORD? (Jer. 37:17).

Nicodemus by night to Jesus:

"How can anyone be born after having grown old? Can one enter a second time into the mother's womb and be born?" (John 3:4).

Pilate in bewilderment to Jesus:

"So you are a king?...What is truth?" (John 18:37–38).

The king said, surely with bestirred wonderment and anxiety:

"Tell me all the great things (*gedolôth*) that Elisha has done."

Israel's testimony in faith specializes in and teems with "great things." Indeed, its entire life and self-announcement of its place in the world are premised on the "great things" of Yahweh. Israel, moreover, has a special and well-developed vocabulary for Yahweh's "great things."

With the same term used here for "great things," Israel celebrates the wonders of Yahweh, both in its history and in the mysterious wonder of creation:

> He is your praise; he is your God, who has done for you these
>   great and awesome things that your own eyes have seen
>   (Deut. 10:21).

> You have done great things,
> O God, who is like you? (Ps. 71:19).

> He does great things and unsearchable, marvelous things
>   without number (Job 5:9; see Ps. 106:21; 111:2).

The "great things" attest to Yahweh's transformative power that is without rival. But Israel, alongside that term used in the question of the king in our text, has other terms for such testimony. The doxological utterance of Psalm 145:4–7 provides an inventory of such terms:

> One generation shall laud your works to another,
>   and shall declare our mighty acts.

On the glorious splendor of your majesty,
and on your wondrous works, I will meditate.
The might of your awesome deeds shall be proclaimed,
and I will declare your greatness.
They shall celebrate the fame of your abundant goodness,
and shall sing aloud of your righteousness.

This psalm, which remains in the sphere of creation as distinct from "historical saving deeds," attests to Yahweh's generous, attentive, sustaining, nourishing, protective care for all creatures. We may pay attention, in turn, to the several terms utilized to allude to and attest Yahweh's "great things":

Works (*ma'asôth*):

For you, O LORD, have made me glad by your work;
at the works of your hands I sing for joy.
How great are your works, O LORD!
Your thoughts are very deep! (Ps. 92:45; see Ps. 33:4; 66:3;
86:8; 103:22; 104:24; 118:17; 143:5. And see in our lead
psalm, Ps. 145, vv. 10, 17.)

Mighty acts *(giborah),* deeds of great power:

I will come praising the mighty deeds of the Lord GOD,
I will praise your righteousness, yours alone (Ps. 71:16).

Praise him for his mighty deeds;
praise him according to his surpassing greatness (Ps. 150:2;
see Ps. 20:7; 106:2, and in Ps. 145, v. 12).

Wondrous works *(niphle'oth),* surpassing expectation:

I will give thanks to the LORD with my whole heart;
I will tell of all your wonderful deeds (Ps. 9:1).

We give thanks to you, O God...
People tell of your wondrous deeds (Ps. 75:1; see Ex. 3:20;
Judg. 6:13; Ps. 26:7; 72:18; 78:11; 105:2).

Awesome deeds *(nor'othoth):*

Say to God, "How awesome are your deeds!
Because of your great power, your enemies cringe before
you..."

Come and see what God has done:
he is awesome in his deeds among mortals (Ps. 66:3,
5; see 2 Sam. 7:23; Isa. 64:2; Ps. 106:22).[4]

Now this rather extended and detailed list of verbs for Yahweh's wondrous acts of power and transformation is something of a digression from our narrative analysis. I make the digression simply to call attention to the fact that Old Testament testimony has a rich vocabulary for Yahweh's transformative acts in "nature and history." When a community has a rich and varied vocabulary for a topic, it indicates that the topic is a specialization in the community that requires carefully nuanced word usage. That is, Israel in its references to Yahweh is in "the miracle business." Its doxological discourse is permeated by reference to transformative acts that are beyond explanation, undeniably concrete, and gladly assigned to Yahweh. This is the core subject matter of Israel's theological-hymnic discourse.

What interests me in our narrative text, in this brief third scene that features a conversation between the king and Gehazi, is that the king says to Gehazi, "Tell me about the *gedolôth* that Elisha has performed." So far as I can determine, this is the only usage of the term "great things" that has a human subject. That is, Elisha is the one, the only one in Israel, well beyond Moses or Elijah, who does transformative acts of power that Israel elsewhere characteristically refers only to Yahweh. The only term used is *gedolôth*, but we may imagine the force of the question, taken theologically, if we extrapolate the entire vocabulary of wonder—works, mighty acts, wondrous works, awesome deeds—and imagine them all assigned to Elisha, this human agent in whom Israel has witnessed the strange power of Yahweh concretely in effect.

The king asks about this unparalleled human wonder worker: "Tell me, I pray." Narrate the story to me. Gehazi, in response, is a willing teller. He is ready to narrate, to tell, he is the reteller of what he has seen and what is remembered in Israel. He is the evangelist, the relater of this good news, the preacher.

He has available—that is, Israel in its canonical way has available—a full inventory of "great things" whereby Elisha has humanly performed the wonders of Yahweh. The bulk of material about Elisha in 2 Kings 3–9 is a list of "great things." We need not enumerate them all, even though Gehazi had them all at his canonical finger-tips; we may simply recount the brief list in chapter 4:

- vv. 1–7: Elisha provided oil for a bereft widow, enough to let her pay her debts;
- vv. 8–17: Elisha gave to the Shunammite woman, the one in this text, at the suggestion of Gehazi, a son when she had none;
- vv. 18–37: Elisha raised the dead son of the woman to new life;
- vv. 38–41: Elisha purified the pot and ended the deathly threat of bad food;
- vv. 42–44: Elisha fed a hundred people with a small amount of food, and had a surplus when he finished.

This series of five acts in one chapter is extraordinary. Any one of these acts is enough to dazzle the community, and to keep the community dazzled over time in its endless retelling. What they saw and remembered and retold is that this Elisha was a bearer of the uncommon power of Yahweh, in completely human form, to enact Yahweh's will for life in the face of the terrifying power of death. What Yahweh has undertaken characteristically in the great acts centering in the Exodus is endlessly retold in story and song. And now, in this local human agent, that same power for life is seen to be operative. Gehazi has all of this available in response to the question of the king.

But kings are busy, and they have short attention spans. Therefore, Gehazi quickly settles on one "great thing" which is a representative summary and epitome of the whole memory. The initial telling in chapter 4 had taken nineteen verses. But the king must be brief and to the point. So the servant summarizes the "great things" about which the king has asked, all nineteen verses reduced in Hebrew to four words:

Introduction: While he was telling the king...

Substance: How Elisha enlivened (the) dead (one)...

That is all he gets to say. A lifetime of inexplicable miracles rendered in four words. It is not even a complete sentence. It is a dependent clause completely lacking in specificity. Missing are the name of the mother, the name of the boy, the cause of death, the method of restoration. Everything missing except the brute, quick claim of the causative verb: "He enlivened," he gave life back ("brought again our Lord Jesus Christ from the dead"; cf. 2 Cor. 4:14; Hebr. 13:20). In that simple utterance Gehazi answered two things to the king: One, that there is power for new life available and death need not prevail. Two, this power for new life is the gift of at least this one human being in the king's realm.

Perhaps Gehazi was only warming to his retelling to the king that might have been more substantive. Maybe he intended to detail the wonder of the restoration of the woman's son. Perhaps if he had been given time, he would have proceeded to other elements of the narrative. But that was all he got to say. He was abruptly cut off in mid-sentence as he uttered the initial dependent clause. By his fourth word, the king's aide had entered the room. He said to the king, "There is a call you have to take; it is urgent and will not wait." Perhaps the king said, "It will have to wait, I am busy. You know Gehazi; he is about to tell me a remarkable tale."

But before the king could say more and before the aide could respond, the woman came barging into the king's office. She entered with a narrative signal: "Behold." She did not wait for protocol. She was not awed by royal furnishings or royal procedures. She was urgent in her own need; her own need disrupted and overrode the conversation of king and servant. Thus, the scene of paced royal conversation is left unfinished, broken off in mid-sentence by this woman with her urgent, passionate demand for restoration. Perhaps it is like that: We are ready to bear witness to the transformative power of life among us. But our telling is interrupted by the entry of the bruised brokenness of real life.

A Royal Verdict

We arrive, finally, at the concluding scene in verses 5–6. Everything now changes with the intrusion of the woman. She has been absent in what I have called the third scene (vv. 4–5a); but we remember her vividly from the earlier lines in the narrative. She is the one, due to the famine and her long absence from the land, who came to have nothing and who promptly filed a legal complaint with the king concerning her lost property, her house and her field.

In this fourth scene, the second scene of "outcry" is resumed. We are told, as she barged into the royal presence, that she "appealed" (cried out) directly to the king. We are not told what she said, but surely she told the king about her absence, her loss, her entitlement, and her indignant expectation. As an aside, Gehazi whispers to the king, "Here is the woman about whom I was telling you...She has been the recipient of and the concrete evidence for the prophetic 'great thing' about which I was speaking when she entered." She apparently brought her son with her, the indisputable evidence of the great thing. She brought her son along as evidence. Perhaps he also represents the stark contrast of Elisha's gift of new life and her current economic crisis that is at the edge of death. The son never speaks. He does not need to speak. He is never described but only mentioned. He does not need to be described. It is enough that he is there, visible to the king. His very presence attests to the king that in the world where Yahweh's new power for life is so concretely evident, old-fashioned, conventional, deathly economics are simply inappropriate and cannot be endured. The very physical presence of the son warns the king about everything old and invites the king to new actions appropriate to the world-defining significance of the "great things."

The rest of the narrative concerns the response of the king to this freighted moment of encounter with prophetic newness that is here embodied. First, the king interviews the woman to get the facts of the case. No doubt she retold to him all the data of verses 1–3, that she had left town at the behest of Elisha due to the famine, and that she came back to nothing. When the king has secured the necessary data, he gives a directive to his aide, a decision concerning the settlement of her suit. It is a final royal verdict in verse 6:

> Restore all that was hers, together with all the revenue of the fields from the day that she left the land until now.

Everything has been moving toward this generous verdict. The king is the only one who can act, for he has all the power. The woman is vulnerable and in deep need. Gehazi has no authority at all, and Elisha is absent from the room. We may observe four features of this royal verdict:

1. The king has power to act, to reassign and redeploy property. Presumably, in the royal system, the king could do this, whether her property had devolved to the crown or to someone else. The narrative account of the property of Mephibosheth and King David's resolve of

that land is ample evidence of the royal capacity concerning land (2 Sam. 9:1–13; 16:1–4; 19:24–30). This of course is what so angers Ahab and Jezebel when their like-royal privilege is thwarted by an old covenantal theory of land (1 Kings 21). It can be argued that in our case the king utilizes his royal capacity precisely to enact the old covenantal practice whereby the woman cannot be separated from her land by sharp commercial dealings. This case then stands in sharp contrast with the Naboth case.

2. The king uses his peculiar authority over land, without reservation, on her behalf. He utters the remarkable verb "restore." Make it as it was before. Too much should not be made of it, but it is this same verb that is used, characteristically, in Jeremiah and Ezekiel to mark the restoration of Judah's destiny and return to the land (Jer. 29:14; 30:3, 18; 31:23; 32:44). It is, moreover, the verb used in Job 42:10 to signal the full restoration of all that Job had lost. This woman in an understated way is a representative characteristic figure for Israel and, derivatively, for all those who have lost everything and receive everything back in ways that make new life possible. She is indeed Israel come back to its full, God-promised inheritance. The king is a player in a drama larger than he knows.

3. What she receives back is her land and her field, full, material, economic restoration. The famine had been severe, and she had been gone seven years. And now she has been given her land back. This is her mini-Jubilee enacted by the king, in recognition (a) that the land is inalienably hers, and (b) she belongs inalienably upon her land and she cannot live without it. The king, in his brief dictum, is an enactment of Israel's deepest conviction about the land of promise as inheritance. These terms—promise, inheritance—so familiar to us, are not just large slogans for theological talk; they matter for the deployment of concrete political, economic power in the service of a vision of social reality. The king exercises no prerogative for his own gain but makes himself a ready agent of a humane, covenantal vision of reality whereby land-givers stand in solidarity with land-needers.

4. The last phrase of the king's verdict is perhaps the most surprising. The king makes the woman's recovery of the land retroactive, so that she is entitled by royal decree to all the produce and revenue that the land generated during her seven-year absence. It is common for

governments to collect "back taxes." It is much less common for governments to guarantee "back revenues" when they have flowed in the other direction. The woman departs the king's chambers fully satisfied. We are not told what Gehazi thought as he observed the stunning scene. Perhaps he noticed that the king's action was not unlike what Elisha himself had characteristically done in such cases where restoration was required.

The Power behind the King

Though quite brief, this is a most peculiar narrative, because its parts seem to be disjointed. The first part concerning the woman's departure and loss and the final part on the woman's recovery fit together as exile and restoration, death and new life. But the middle section concerning the conversation of king and servant, without inclusion of the woman, is very strange, capped by the complete absence of Elisha himself, once the narrative gets under way.

When I ask about the interrelatedness of the parts and how the story works—or is intended to work—I suggest the following that yields something like a clue to missional engagement or more concretely, a theology of preaching. The exchange at the center of the narrative in verses 4–5a designates Gehazi as the teller, the reteller of what he has heard and seen, as the one who gives testimony about Elisha and his actions that have taken place elsewhere, in another time, another place, and in other circumstances. What his testimony does is to certify to the king that the king's own realm is an arena for the "great things" enacted humanly.

The leap from this half-completed conversation is abrupt. Nothing is said that suggests a connection between Gehazi's testimony to the king and the king's generous action toward the needy woman. But it is certain that talk of concrete "great things," humanly performed, is still ringing in the ears of the king when he interviews the woman and when he determines her legitimate entitlements.

We may well ask why the king acted as he did. He did not need to act in this way; in general kings are not known for such solidarity with the needy vulnerable. The Omride kings, moreover, have no such reputation and this is, after all, a son of Ahab. The king could have brushed her off and refused the case. He could have shrewdly calculated that if he restored her land, the act would entail either direct economic loss to the crown or an affront to some powerful family that had confiscated the land. Either way, restoration of land to the woman might readily have been seen as a liability to the throne. Plus the fact that every such royal decision sets a visible precedent that invites many other like suits. The narrative is too terse to reflect on all this; but we should notice that the king's action is not normal. It is, rather, a remarkable act of generous attentiveness to need, not what is expected of a son of Ahab, especially if we compare this to the account of Naboth's vineyard.

In an attempt to understand this peculiar narrative, I propose the following: the story is designed to suggest that the testimony of Elisha's "great things" functions as an impetus for the king's remarkable action. Recital of "great things," the *giving of testimony*, evokes *new royal possibility* whereby the king steps out of his accustomed behavior that is characteristically self-serving; he himself enacts a "great thing." He restores land to a bereft woman. His "great thing" (which replicates the "great things" of Elisha that in turn shadow the "great things" of Yahweh) is to give the gift of socioeconomic possibility to one without resources. This is a "great thing" because it is an act of concrete solidarity that inconveniences and costs the king, but gives new life to one of his subjects. The "great thing" of the king is not elaborate or dramatic, for the "great thing" of such authority figures—unlike that of visionaries and poets—takes place in the day-to-day performances of administrative duties that entail the management of money, property, land, and people.

I believe, nonetheless, that the king would have been unwilling or unable to take such action had his imagination and self-understanding not been impinged upon in powerful ways by the testimony of good news on the lips of Gehazi, who substantiated quite concretely that the powers of life are indeed on the loose in the world. The king, in a royal, formal, unspectacular way, undertakes a "great thing" that is as life-giving as Elisha's characteristic work and is empowered and informed by this testimony. The enduring, dramatic, compelling power of Elisha is not directly operative in this story. It is operative only at a remove, by the retelling, the "retailing" testimony of Gehazi, who brings the force and authority for newness from the prophet's other venues to this royal venue where the king can operate differently in the wake of Elisha. For one instant, the king catches a glimpse of what his realm would be like were it pervaded by the power and concrete substance of "great things." Moreover, the king makes himself available in this instant for that unlikely possibility. The "double portion" of Elijah's spirit, carried by Elisha, in this moment spills over into a royal decision about land for the woman (see 2 Kings 2:9). Her "cry" receives a royal answer marked by attentive generosity that causes the king to step outside the common royal horizon to work a new thing.

Testimony and Royal Possibility

My pondering of this little narrative has led me to imagine ecclesial futures generated by the memory. It occurred to me that what we see here *in nuce* is *testimony that creates royal possibility*, replicated in a larger way in the book of Acts:

1. This community, like the gift of Elijah to Elisha (and I believe in this case indirectly also to the Omride king), is under *the impetus of the spirit*, powered beyond itself in bold capacities to transform life. It is the spirit clearly operative in the world of Elisha that endlessly propels the church in Acts beyond itself.

2. This powered community gave *testimony* of what it remembered of Jesus that they considered a present-tense claim upon them. It is not too much to say that the preaching of Peter is a recital of "great things" of Yahweh in the history of Israel and then in the life of Jesus. That, of course, is why the book of Acts counts on "the events that have been fulfilled among us" in the book of Luke (Luke 1:1).

3. The recital of great things is made characteristically *in the presence of authorities*, not unlike Gehazi's to the king. Thus, Paul is characteristically before the authorities: before the council, before Felix, before Festus, before Agrippa, all of whom are invited to reconstrue their worlds according to the claim of the "great things" of Jesus. These authorities, unlike the king in our narrative, are "almost persuaded" (Acts 26:28).

4. The recital of great things, powered by the spirit, before the authorities, leads to *dramatic acts* that turn the world upside down:

> When they could not find them, they dragged Jason and some believers before the city authorities, shouting, "These people who have been turning the world upside down have come here also" (Acts 17:6–7).

The church attested that "there is another way," a message that was, perhaps, clear to Gehazi's king, the one who acted differently in a new obedience.

Transformative Testimony

If it is the case, as I think, that our narrative pivots on the brief, unfinished testimony of Gehazi, then the act of testimony is urgently constitutive of the new world authorized by our narrative.[5] Where there is no testimony to "great things," women without land are hopeless and kings can proceed in their self-interest without ever considering otherwise. The power of testimony, however, alights right in the corridors of power to assert that the world is not closed according to the royal status quo arrangements of property and control. As related by Gehazi, Elisha insists that it could be otherwise. Not always, but from time to time such a claim, when verbalized, yields altered policy that makes things new. We have no indication that the king was very reflective. He was not exuberant about Gehazi's testimony, nor did he explain his own subsequent action to the astonished narrator. He simply did "the right thing." Such imaginative acts of policy that bespeak transformative solidarity, acts that occur only occasionally, are compelling evidence that the practice of testimony is crucial and worth doing. Testimony is the way in which remembered miracles have durable, present-tense power.[6] Even in the understatement of this brief narrative, half a sentence of testimony, before the petitioner comes into the royal chamber, makes a decisive difference in the notice of the vulnerable and the management of power.

6

The Overstated Prophetic "Or"

1 Kings 20:1–43

The imaginative "or" of prophetic faith is absolutist in its demand and uncompromising in its claim. It means, characteristically, to override any possible "either" that envisions life outside of Yahwism and beyond total obedience to Torah. The "otherwise" offered by prophetic faith, as I have indicated, is characteristically poetic and elusive, an invitation beyond concrete life that is in hand. This "otherwise," however, is easily given to an ideological hardening so that a future that is imagined lyrically too readily becomes a totalizing claim that is soon as problematic as the "either" it intends to defeat.

An Absolute "Or"

I shall take up the long narrative of 1 Kings 20 by way of reflecting upon an "or" become impatiently absolute, and an "otherwise" uncompromising in its totalism. This long narrative is rather a neglected orphan text in the larger configuration of prophetic tales. It is essentially a war story; perhaps its usual disregard is due to the fact that it is embedded in the Elijah cycle of narratives, but Elijah is absent from this text. Nor has Elisha yet become active in this narrative, though he is summoned by Elijah in the narrative just preceding this story (1 Kings 19:19–21). There are, to be sure, several prophetic figures active in this narrative, but they are anonymous and seem to play only stereotypical roles. These unnamed prophetic figures are derivative from the community led by Elijah, that is, disciples, and perhaps disciples who lack the greatness of the initiator tend to distort or harden the vision of the leader.

The only reference that is characteristically made to this narrative in the ongoing work of Old Testament interpretation is from Walther Zimmerli, who has attended to the double formula "You shall know that I am the LORD" in verses 13 and 28.[1] Zimmerli believes that this narrative embedment of the formula is at the origin of the trajectory of divine self-announcement that will come to be crucial in the developed tradition of Ezekiel. With reference to this narrative on its own terms, moreover, Zimmerli's focus in the narrative is exactly correct, for it is the intent of this narrative to hold together the sovereign theological claim of Yahweh and the brutalizing victory of war. It is this interface that constitutes the primary claim of the narrative and, eventually, its deep problematic as well.

The context for the war narrative, not surprisingly, is Israel's ongoing conflict with Syria. That hostility was perhaps over disputed territory (as with the Golan Heights) and an unstable boundary between the two states that expanded and retracted territory from one state or the other, depending upon the relative strength of the two states.

The bulk of the text consists in two narrative cycles, each of which is patterned around three themes:

(a) royal posturing and blustering;
(b) prophetic urging and assurance;
(c) battle report.

Added to these two reiterated accounts involving king, prophet, and army in verses 1–21 and verses 22–30a is an addendum in verses 30b–42 that will finally occupy our interest.

War

The first cycle of military narrative is in verses 1–21. At the outset, Ben-hadad, king in Damascus, has organized a huge coalition of city-kings with a great amount of arms that moves to set a siege against the city of Samaria. Along with real military threat is the psychological power of great intimidation from such a vast alliance (v. 1). After the factual report of verse 1, the narrator makes us privy to the negotiations that take place between the two kings. (To see this imagined "transcript" of the exchange is like having access to the White House Tapes of John Kennedy during "the Cuban Missile Crisis," tapes that contain the important, heretofore confidential exchanges with the government of the Soviet Union.)[2]

Ben-hadad is the eager aggressor, who demands from Ahab total unconditional surrender:

> "Your silver and gold are mine; your fairest wives and children also are mine" (v. 3).

Ahab, in a weak situation made weaker by anxiety and unfaith (on which see a parallel in Isa. 7:1–17), readily agrees to the surrender of all his resources, money, and family. Ahab is willing to be totally humiliated in order to save his throne, clearly assuming that he has no alternative to capitulation. From the angle of the narrative, moreover, he had no alternative, because he and his dynastic family had long since forsaken Yahweh, the only saving possibility for the crown.

Emboldened by such shameless appeasement, Ben-hadad adds to his demand and to Ahab's humiliation:

> "I sent to you, saying, 'Deliver to me your silver and gold, your wives and children'; nevertheless I will send my servants to you tomorrow about this time, and they shall search your house and the houses of your servants, and lay hands on whatever pleases them, and take it away." (vv. 5–6)

Ben-hadad will now proceed as if there were no king in Samaria, as if he himself and his troops could loot and plunder at will, completely unrestrained. Thus far Israel and its king are in a completely hopeless situation.

Ahab's throne, however, is not an absolute monarchy. It has long been recognized that the Northern regime in Israel was something of a constitutional monarchy (see 2 Sam. 5:1–5). For that reason the king must consult with village elders, who act as a restraint on royal willfulness, and here, on royal cowardice. Ahab must report to the elders on his readiness to comply with Syria's savage demands. The elders, however, are made of tougher fiber than is the king and are in no mood for appeasement; they refuse to sanction such total surrender.

They are prepared for war and ready to resist the threat of Syria as the king was not. At the direction of the elders, who have vetoed his policy of appeasement, Ahab sends his response to the Syrian king: Ahab will accept the first demand of money and family to which he has already agreed; he will not, however, accept the second demand that the Syrians should run loose in Samaria, looting and plundering (v. 9). He will not accede to the complete collapse of social order for which he has royal responsibility.

Now the die is cast and the calculus of demand and compliance is determined. Syria has demanded more than Israel will grant. War has become inevitable. All that remains is exaggerated diplomatic rhetoric in which each side voices bravado.

Ben-hadad:

"The gods do so to me, and more also, if the dust of Samaria will provide a handful for each of the people who follow me" (v. 10). [So many Syrians!]

Ahab:

"Tell him: One who puts on armor should not brag like one who takes it off" (v. 11).

Each treats the other with dismissive contempt, no doubt to enliven "the war effort" at home. The narrative then quickly reports, at the end of the rhetorical contest, that the Syrian king has been drinking; in his drunkenness he (unwisely?) orders mobilization for the siege of Samaria (v. 12). This notice is a final effort of the Israelite narrator to deride the Syrian king. The rhetoric has ended with the king's blustering. For all his bravado at the behest of his elders, Ahab would seem to be in a weak, if not hopeless military situation, surely reflected in his initial concession to Syria.

After twelve verses of royal exchange, however, the scene changes (vv. 13–14). Now, with an opening *hinneh*, "one of the prophets" comes to Ahab. He comes with an oracle from Yahweh:

Have you seen all this great multitude? Look, I will give it into your hand today; and you shall know that I am the LORD (v. 13).

The "great multitude" of thirty-two city-kings—alluded to by Ben-hadad in verse 10—now laying siege to Samaria will be defeated; by the Israelite victory Yahweh will be recognized as sovereign. Thus the old "Yahweh versus Baal" contest of chapters 18—19 (with Ahab on the wrong side) draws Yahweh into the battle in order to exhibit incomparable power and authority. The prophet identifies the troops who will do the fighting. When the king inquires, "Who shall begin the battle?" the anonymous prophet says tersely to the king, "You" (v. 14).

We have in turn royal posturing (vv. 1–12) and prophetic assurance (vv. 13–14), which is also a form of posturing—divine posturing! Now follows the battle report (vv. 15–21). Ahab may be weak and cowardly but, as the prophet has anticipated, the weakness and cowardice of Ahab do not count in the face of Yahweh's own resolve. In the battle report itself, Yahweh does not figure. This is real war that entails real risk and that eventuates in real killing and real dying. Even so, the outcome is not in doubt. Syria is routed, the king of Syria flees, and Israel wins a great victory.

> Each killed his man; the Arameans fled and Israel pursued them, but King Ben-hadad of Aram escaped on a horse with the cavalry. The king of Israel went out, attacked the horses and chariots, and defeated the Arameans with a great slaughter (vv. 20–21).

The great victory is there for all to see, Israel and Syria. But only those who heard the prophet, that is, only those who have the text with the prophetic announcement, know the true tale of the war. While the war appears to be "Syria versus Israel," or even Ben-hadad in his drunkenness versus Ahab in his cowardice, such a reading of the war misses the point. The narrative clearly pivots on the prophetic assurance. At the heart of the prophetic assurance is the claim of Yahweh: "You shall know." Now Israel knows. Israel knows that Yahweh is the key player in its life. Ahab and all his contemporaries now know that Yahweh matters decisively. Ahab and all those who come after him know that in the midst of drunkenness and cowardice, in the midst of surrender and resistance, in the midst of bombast and much killing, it is all Yahweh. Yahweh's visible presence in the narrative is confined to the two verses of prophetic utterance. The discerning reader, however, knows that Yahweh is present everywhere in the narrative, surely present in the battle report of victory, likely present in the preliminaries that show Ahab to be dysfunctional. Yahweh is present and decisive, even if unseen and unacknowledged by most.

The assurance is, "You shall acknowledge." That is the point of it all. The war serves to give glory to Yahweh, glory that means practical, concrete, political enhancement that enlarges Yahweh's realm and splendor over all other rivals (see Ex. 14:4, 17; Isa. 42:8; 48:11).

More War

The problem with the diplomacy of violence is that wars do not stay won, even if won by Yahweh. Certainly in the case of Syria versus Israel, the victory of Israel assured no future. And therefore the entire pattern of royal posturing, prophetic assurance, and battle report must be done all over a second time—done in a way to permit the narrator to exhibit formidable rhetorical skills, done in a way to manifest Yahweh's decisive governance (vv. 22–30a). In this second time round, everything is escalated:

- the royal rhetoric is more extreme;
- the prophetic assurance is more certain,
- the battle is more brutal.

Given the threefold exaggeration, however, the story line remains unchanged. In the purview of the narrator, Yahweh will always finally dominate the story line and the battle.

In this second narrative sequence, "the prophet" appears at the outset in order to introduce the drama to follow (v. 22). He does so by a declaration to Ahab that Israel must again prepare for war, for in the spring Syria will attack again (see 2 Sam. 11:1). The prophetic announcement need not be regarded as the work of a seer who can foresee the future. It could be simply a shrewd analysis of international relations. Or it could be, as in 2 Kings 6:8–12, that the prophet has inexplicable penetration into the Syrian intelligence network. In whatever way, the prophet knows. As a consequence, the king of Israel knows, and the narrative may advance.

When we come this time to royal posturing, we do not have, as in the first sequence, Ben-hadad making demands on Israel or mocking the Israelite king. Perhaps the sound defeat he had received indicated a different approach the second time. Less bombast, more careful planning. We have a report on the war council in Damascus, whereby the Syrian king receives advice from his military staff. The counsel of the advisors in verses 23–25 is in two parts, an analysis and a subsequent proposal. The analysis is an assessment of the relative capacity of the two military forces:

Their gods are gods of the hills, and so they were stronger than we (v. 23a).

The judgment is cast as a theological assessment of the relative strength of the gods of Israel and Syria. Likely the theological expression should not be taken too literally or too seriously. It may be that it was a characteristic way of speaking about "strength" that surely was understood always in relation to the gods. Indeed, perhaps the Syrians, if not Ahab, had taken the prophet seriously and had "recognized" Yahweh in the previous victory of Israel. More likely the analysis expressed in theological terms is to be understood as a rhetorical preparation by the narrator for the Israelite response in verse 28, whereby affront is taken by the Israelites, even if not given by the Syrians. In any case, the analysis is a Syrian recognition that Israel's just-completed rout of Syria is the result of fighting on unfriendly terrain that was greatly to the advantage of the hill country people, who were able to use what must have been "guerilla tactics." The advisors recognize that their perhaps more ordered ways of battle (with chariots) will never succeed on such terrain.

And so follows logically the proposed battle plan offered to the king in three parts: First, fight on the plain, not in the hill country, thereby neutralizing the advantage of Israel (and its gods). Second, get better leaders, real military men and not politicians (city-kings). Perhaps the city-kings had been left to lead the battle in verse 1 in order to show the extent of the political alliance. Political leaders who have great symbolic significance for effective intimidation, however, do not do well in actual battle; so replace them! Third, rearm vigorously. All of this is sound military advice. Ben-hadad recognizes it as such and accepts the proposal. Inside the narrative, the purpose of Syrian preparation for battle is to portray Israel's situation as dire, and so prepare for the soon-to-come victory of Yahweh in the face of great odds.

Now comes the first part of the battle report, the establishment of supply lines and selection of a battle site (v. 26). The place chosen is Aphek. Apparently this is a location to the east of the Jordan in territory disputed by the two states, on the main highway that ran between Damascus and Israelite territory. The main point of the locus is that it was on flat plains that voided the Israelite military advantage of hill country fighting at which Syria was not skilled. From an Israelite perspective, then, the staging of the second battle is even more dangerous than the first, with higher risks and longer odds. As Syria positions itself for battle in a rather choreographed procedure, so Israel does likewise. While verses 26–27a are a sober report, in verse 27b the Israelite narrator cannot resist an imaginative metaphor to characterize the context made more ominous by the Syrian-selected terrain:

> The people of Israel encamped opposite them like two little flocks of goats, while the Arameans filled the country.

The imagery not only points to the number of Israelite troops; they are few. It is a small force, grossly outnumbered. But the metaphor deals with more than numbers. By its use of "goats," it portrays Israel as weak and vulnerable, exposed and defenseless. While the term for goat ('z) may bespeak strength, it is most likely here that the term is to be taken as a reference to the condition of a flock that includes both goats and sheep, thus not strength but vulnerability. The missing but implied element in the metaphor is a bear or a lion, ready to swoop down on the defenseless herd. The metaphor, as well as Syria's initial rhetoric in verse 23, is designed to show Israel helpless and at risk.

Such a context of vulnerability, however, is exactly the chosen moment for the reappearance of a prophet, for such inscrutable spokespersons tend to show up at moments when Israel has been pressed beyond its capacity (v. 28). This speaker is termed "man of God." He is, of course, unnamed, and there is no reason to think that this is the same speaker as in verses 13–14, and 22. The point of the narrative is rather that the large scope of royal risk and anxiety is profoundly contradicted by prophetic figures who speak for Yahweh and who regularly show up, albeit unpredictably, to redefine lived reality by reference to Yahweh.

The prophetic oracle from Yahweh is not unlike that of verse 13, except that the rhetoric, congruent with the tone of the second sequence, has been escalated. The main force of the announcement is to assert that Yahweh will again defeat "this great multitude of Syrians." Israel may be exposed and vulnerable, but Yahweh is more than equal to the test and will protect Israel. Again, as in verse 13, the purpose of the victory is that Yahweh will be acknowledged as sovereign. As in verse 13, nothing is said of Yahweh's commitment to Israel. Rather it is that Yahweh's own status will be enhanced by the victory in the eyes of Israel as in the eyes of the Syrians. As in Ezekiel 36:22–32, moreover, Yahweh's only method for self-enhancement is to win a victory that, as a by-product but not the main point, is beneficial for Israel as well. The importance of Yahweh's self-enhancement and the fuller acknowledgement of Yahweh's sovereignty, however, are more urgent in context. The prophetic speaker skillfully takes the analysis made by Syrian military men in verse 23 and converts that conventional rhetoric about "the gods of the hills" into a mocking theological taunt, when in fact the Syrians had made a stone-cold sober, unemotional, certainly non-theological use of the phrasing. Now the prophet turns the rhetoric against Syria in order to motivate and rescue Israel.

Because:

The Arameans have said, "The Lord is a god of the hills but he is not a god of the valleys,"

therefore:

I will give all this great multitude into your hand, and you shall know that I am the LORD (v. 28).

The "slander" of Yahweh by the Syrians is turned to motivation for Israel. Yahweh had perhaps not been mocked by the Syrian commanders who had no theological axe to grind, but "Yahweh will not be mocked" (see 2 Kings 19:4, 16). Indeed the prayer of Hezekiah is nicely parallel to our prophetic oracle, for his prayer also turns mocking to motivation:

O LORD the God of Israel, who are enthroned above the cherubim, you are God, you alone, of all the kingdoms of the earth; you have made heaven and earth. Incline your ear, O LORD, and hear; open your eyes, O LORD, and see; hear the words of Sennacherib, which he has sent to mock the living God. Truly, O LORD, the kings of Assyria have laid waste the nations and their lands, and have hurled their gods into the fire, though they were no gods but the work of human hands—wood and stone—and so they were destroyed. So now, O LORD our God, save us, I pray you, from his hand, so that all the kingdoms of the earth may know that you, O LORD, are God alone. (2 Kings 19:16–19)

The conclusion, yet again, is that all will know (acknowledge) Yahweh as God alone. A military contest is turned to a great theological crisis.

Finally in this sequence, the completion of the battle report is continued from verses 26–27 (vv. 29–30a). The battle was fierce and lasted seven long days. But the outcome was never in doubt:

> The Israelites killed one hundred thousand Aramean foot soldiers in one day. The rest fled into the city of Aphek; and the wall fell on twenty-seven thousand men that were left (vv. 29–30a).

What a slaughter: 100,000 Syrian foot soldiers on one day, plus 27,000 crushed by the city wall of Aphek where they had fled in retreat! It is an immense slaughter, utterly one-sided. We do not hear the number of Israelite casualties. Are they so small as to be negligible? The important point is that Yahweh is as good as Yahweh's word. Yahweh has prevailed. It turns out that Yahweh is a "God of the plains," as effective there as in the hill country, effective everywhere, before whom no people and no other god have a chance.

Yahweh has, characteristically, worked an immense and otherwise inexplicable inversion. Ahab has been a coward with no chance of winning. Israel has been like a flock of exposed goats, sure to be devoured. But it all goes the other way. The narrative is in no doubt that Yahweh is the single cause of victory and defeat. The whole has been a demonstration of Yahweh's unchallenged sovereignty, here enacted in solidarity with Israel. It is all Yahweh, only Yahweh. We never hear from Ahab on the point, either to doubt the claim of Yahweh or to embrace it. He could not, in any case, have missed the point. His life, the life of his people, and the security of his throne are all an unwarranted gift of Yahweh. Without Yahweh, the entire enterprise would be eaten alive as a defenseless goat. But Yahweh has spoken and Yahweh has acted. The body count in Syria is nearly unbearable, all attestation to Yahweh.

Diplomacy after War

But now, after these great public events, we come in the remainder of our story to a personal, intimate, face-to-face transaction (vv. 30a–43). In the first battle, the defeated Ben-hadad, now no doubt sobered up from his drinking, escaped on a horse—just barely (v. 20). He rode away with his cavalry. Presumably his royal identity was still intact, for he was accompanied by his bodyguard. Now we are to consider his escape from the second, more severe defeat. This time the defeat is more massive, and the danger to the defeated king is surely more palpable. This time there is no horse, no cavalry, no bodyguard, none of the visible trappings of his royal office. His escape is now less glorious, completely inappropriate to a king. We are told simply, "He fled," presumably alone, abandoned (v. 30). He entered Samaria to hide. He is nothing more than a desperate fugitive, so complete is Israel's victory, so effective is Yahweh's assurance. But this is in fact an ex-king, for the real King, Yahweh, has won the day. We are led to the detail of royalty now abased, even as Yahweh has been glorified. The narrative of total defeat and total victory leave no doubt that the Syrians had made a bad theological calculation. It turns out that "the god of the hills" does very well in the plains. Yahweh is a God of the plains as well, before whom the Syrian gods are helpless. The narrator, however, is markedly restrained. He makes no point of Yahweh's victory. The victory no doubt speaks for itself and requires no interpretive comment. This leaves the narrator free to turn from victorious Yahweh to humiliated, jeopardized Ben-hadad. He sneaks into Samaria, the city to which the victorious God Yahweh is attached.

Now follows a carefully choreographed meeting between Ahab the victor and Ben-hadad the loser (vv. 31–34). The meeting is arranged by Ben-hadad's faithful advisors. They had heard that the kings in Israel practice covenantal fidelity (*hesed*). I am not sure where they had heard that, as we have no report to suggest that. It is true that David, the father of all kings in Israel, is indeed a man of *hesed* who honors promises made (see 1 Sam. 20:14–17; 2 Sam. 9:1; 10:2). In any case, the non-Israelites have the hope and impression that *hesed* operates in royal Israel. Ben-hadad has no alternative, and so the appeal is worth a chance. His advisors, appropriately dressed as submissive losers, approach Ahab: "Let me live."

Ahab responds as they had hoped, generously: "He is my brother." Ahab expresses his solidarity with the king he has defeated. On technical grounds this may mean that the two states, under the two dynasties, have old treaty understandings that even the war does not disrupt, and that Ahab will honor the older, durable understandings. Or it might be that "brother talk" means that there is indeed an informal fraternity among kings. Ahab understands that Ben-hadad's aggressiveness toward Israel was "just business," nothing personal, so that it does not need to evoke in Ahab any enduring hostility or resentment. Either way, Ahab draws a line against further vengeful hostility toward Syria. One may recognize in this decision a wise (or shrewd) political awareness that master politicians practice, knowing that "post-war" reconstruction will require living with Syrians who will not go away, even in defeat. It is important to recognize that Ahab's verdict is the pragmatic wisdom of a durable government that refuses a killer instinct in the service of the durable realities of politics. It could be taken as magnanimity, but I suspect it is practical and realistic.

The verdict of Ahab is reported to Ben-hadad by his men. Ben-hadad, hearing the good news that he is not a "wanted man" in Samaria, goes to Ahab. His antagonist is now to be his rescuer and senior partner in a freshly asserted alliance. He comes to Ahab in a chariot, yet one semblance of royal power. He rides in the last limousine left to the vanquished. And when he arrives without any bargaining power, he immediately makes two crucial concessions to Ahab that were perhaps the issues of the war:

(a) He will restore territory. The term "restore" is the same that the king uses for the Shunammite woman in 2 Kings 8:6, and surely refers to the land east of the Jordan in endless dispute between the two states, something like the Golan Heights (see 9:11–13 for a like transaction).

(b) He grants Ahab trading privileges in Damascus, the establishment of an Israelite franchise in the Damascus mall. As always, wars are about *land and trade*. Ben-hadad wisely concedes the contested points.

In response, Ahab generously accepts the terms (v. 34). His response indicates that his initial generosity toward Ben-hadad was not unconditional charity, but depended upon the terms of settlement. Ahab does not want to kill or to scorch the earth of Syria. He wants land and trade, and now he has both. He has not only succeeded in battle, but he has won the peace.

The settlement is practical and pragmatic, and makes punishment of the conquered king both unnecessary and irrelevant to the future. By this concession on the part of Ben-hadad, Ahab is able to "normalize" relations with Syria and its governing dynasty:

I will let you go on those terms (*berîth*). So he made a treaty (*berîth*) with him and let him go (v. 34).

The double use of the term *berîth* picks up on *hesed* in verse 31 and *brother* in verse 32. We need not romanticize. These are practical men doing business. Enmity extends only to reasons of state; when reasons of state are satisfied, enmity may yield to complete normalization. Ben-hadad is defeated; he has consequently surrendered territory and has yielded on trade provisions. But he is still king and is no longer under threat. Ahab has acted, albeit belatedly, courageously and finally wisely…which turns out to be generously. He has made a peace quite advantageous to his state. He has achieved the goals of diplomacy via war.

Prophecy after War

Here the narrative would end, if the narrative were a royal record. This is not, however, a royal record. This is a prophetic narrative in the midst of other prophetic narratives. We have already seen the decisive impact of prophetic utterance on royal policy in verses 13–14, 22, and 28. The endless accent of these anonymous prophets is that Yahweh is the key player in royal policy. Victory will come in order that Yahweh should be singularly acknowledged.

As the prophetic figures evoke war, it is inevitable that they should now reengage in the narrative after victory in terms of the management of the peace (vv. 35–43). This final paragraph of the narrative shows prophetic passion impinging upon royal pragmatism. The entire scenario, we are told, happens at the command of Yahweh (v. 35). The God who has won the victory is the God who now intrudes afresh into royal settlement. First the narrative reports on an internal prophetic transaction of a very odd kind (vv. 35–38). Prophetic figure A, at Yahweh's command, orders prophetic figure B to beat up on him. The latter refuses, and is promptly devoured by a lion, a recurring enforcer of Yahweh's odd will. Second, having disposed of the recalcitrant prophetic figure B, prophetic figure A now goes to prophetic figure C, and commands him to beat him up. Unlike prophetic figure B, who refused and was devoured, prophetic figure C obeys and beats up on prophetic figure A, injuring him enough so that he must wear all kinds of bandages and have the appearance of a victim of war violence. The elaborate prophetic charade—street theatre—is all preparation for an encounter with the unsuspecting king.

Now, in verses 39–43, the king approaches and is confronted by the prophet. Prophetic figure A, now bandaged and disguised, continues his charade with the king. He pretends (that is, lies to the king at the behest of Yahweh) that he was to guard a Syrian prisoner of war during the combat. Through carelessness, the lie continues, he permitted the prisoner to escape, even though he had been warned that the escape of this prisoner would lead to his own loss of life, "a life for a life." The fictive scenario is constructed for the king and presented to the king, even though no question about the imagined case is voiced to the king. We are to understand, though it is only implied, that the king is being asked to rule on the fate of the negligent guard. The prophetic figure has made the case acute by presenting himself as the failed, guilty party. The king, final arbiter in such cases, does not rule and need not rule. The king simply observes to the prophet that the penalty is already given in the case: "You," you fictive perpetrator, are guilty. You know you deserve the penalty, and the king does not need to say more. The laconic response of the king is not unlike Jesus in Mark 10:19. No new verdict is required; the point is self-evident.

Now, in an abrupt disclosure, the prophetic figure removes his bandages. The king recognizes him immediately as one of the endlessly troublesome prophets of the company of Elijah. In verse 41, without anything being spoken, the king can immediately see what has happened. Through an elaborate deception, the king has been drawn into a self-indictment not unlike that of David in 2 Samuel 12:1–5. The ruse of the prophet is a parable that in an abrupt moment of recognition becomes fully clear:

The escaped prisoner of war is Ben-hadad;

The careless guard who permitted escape is Ahab himself.

The careless guard has let the prisoner escape and stands under penalty of "a life for a life." In this parabolic threat, Ahab stands under a death penalty. All of that is immediately clear in verse 41, both to the king and to the reader. Then follows in official formulation a prophetic speech of judgment against the king:

indictment: *because* you have let the man go who was devoted to destruction;

sentence: *therefore* your life shall be for his life and your people for his people.

Two observations are in order on this prophetic utterance. First, in the indictment the prophet uses the old, harsh term, "devoted to destruction" (*herem*). The king of Syria was under "ban," to be obliterated as a sign of total commitment to Yahweh. The *herem* was commanded as the ideological foundation of total war in complete allegiance to Yahweh. Ahab, in letting Ben-hadad go home alive, has compromised radical Yahwism. This is the same violation Saul, his antecedent in the north, had committed with the Amalekites, an act that cost Saul his throne (1 Sam. 15). Like Saul, like Ahab.

Second, in the sentence, the prophet has extended the harsh punishment for the life of the king to the life of the entire northern community, thus anticipating the destruction of the entire northern kingdom to come only a century later. In both the *herem* of judgment and the extrapolation of the sentence, the prophet has pushed the speech of judgment to its furthest extremity, turning the pragmatic settlement of the king into a demonic disobedience.

It is no wonder that the king does not respond at all to the prophetic trick in verse 43. He is speechless after having acted, we would say, courageously and wisely on behalf of his realm. He is stunned and defeated. His reaction is to go home "resentful and sullen," the same phrasing he will have in 21:4 in the next narrative when Naboth will not yield to him. Ahab is exhausted by and resourceless against the old, passionate requirements and insistences of the prophet that are rooted in the most elemental commitments of old-fashioned, simplistic Yahwism. The king who had decisively won the day for Samaria, by the end of the war narrative, has been completely defeated by the old traditions and left spent and crushed. The king can manage an army; he is, however, powerless before the savage work of the prophet who flattens all the complexities of public life into a simple "either/or."

When "Either/Or" Should Be "Both/And"

Our theme throughout these narratives has been the "imagined or" of the prophetic, which by speech and action generates an "otherwise" that will not be tamed to or controlled by the royal horizon. We have watched that "or" emerge in powerful and stunning ways:

- in the relentless ministry of Elijah, who will come soon again;
- in leprosy turned to baby flesh for the Syrian general;
- in gospel bread given via lepers in the face of famine; and
- in prophetic "great things" that invite the king to do a "great thing" for the restoration of the woman.

The sympathy of the narrator is completely on the side of the prophetic "or" that aims to override the royal "either" of leprosy, of land loss, or of famine. The sympathy of this interpreter, like almost every interpreter, is for the prophetic "otherwise," knowing that the "otherwise" Yahweh will yet give in Yahweh's always near-coming realm is a joy beyond the present. None can doubt that the tradition moves in that welcome direction of "otherwise," by both text and interpretation.

This present narrative, however, invites a sober caution in our appreciation of prophetic zeal. In this text, as I read it, Ahab the king has acted practically, honorably, and sensibly, in order to focus energy upon present-tense, post-war, legitimate sociopolitical realities. Ahab must govern in a less-than-perfect world. He must govern in a world where Syrian power is durable and resistant. He must govern where competing trade interests produce trade wars and where territorial disputes require tenuous and provisional settlements. He must live in a "Niebuhrian" world of practical public realities that are not susceptible to power settlements, for power settlements with winner-take-all would simply prepare for the next round of blood-letting that is sure to come in a no-compromise world. He is a compromiser, as a power broker will be and must be. His compromise is to let the Syrian king live. His compromise is to acknowledge that Syrians are real people with brotherly rights, and therefore the rights to trade and land (and perhaps water) must be negotiated. Without undue applause for Ahab, his post-war agreement with Ben-hadad secured what was needed for reasons of state without opening the door for the seeds of future vengeance.

That compromise, however, is precisely the point at issue with the prophet. The prophet has escalated the compromise. Now it is not "Ahab versus Ben-hadad" or "Israel versus Syria." Now it is "Yahweh versus Baal." The inescapable *relativity* of socioeconomic-political-military matters is invested with theological *absoluteness* that admits of no compromise, but that insists upon winner-take-all brutality that has no interest in living together tomorrow.

The key to the theological absoluteness that this street theatre introduces against the realism of royal policy is carried in the word *herem*. [3] The term and its brutal ideology had long since disappeared from the Israelite horizon as Israel had set about building a state among other states. (So David in 1 Sam. 30.) Indeed, it can be argued that it is exactly state-building among other states that had caused Ahab to stop short of killing Ben-hadad and to permit him to go missing.

But unlike everyone else in Israel, these radical prophets have very old memories. They forget nothing, not even a word like *herem*. They forgive nothing, certainly not any royal compromise. They insist that the old, simplest ideological version of Yahwism, of the most brutal kind, must be practiced, no matter the circumstance. In their eyes, as Philip Stern suggests, the release of Ben-hadad is not a realistic political act, but a huge theological sell-out. According to verses 13 and 28, it is Yahweh only who is to receive attention, and so Ben-hadad must "belong" to Yahweh. By releasing the Syrian king, Ahab seems to think that Ben-hadad is his to dispose of as he chooses, his rather than Yahweh's. The singular proprietary claim of Yahweh is taken to be violated by the king; thus the sweeping sentence on Ahab and his realm.

The prophet is clearly unable to consider what futures are to be generated by such an act as that of Ahab. Indeed, a winner-take-all ideology is incapable of thinking clearly about the future, because everything is to be settled in this poignant moment of absoluteness, this present moment taken to be of cosmic proportion. The careful futures of land and trade negotiated by Ahab in his settlement count for nothing in this one-dimensional scenario that has such compelling religious tone to it.

Of course, a case can be made for the singular "or" of a prophetic exclusionary insistence. Such a radicality as that voiced by the prophet evokes important sympathy among us. This narrative, however, invites us to observe that there come times, occasions, and circumstances when the radicality of "or," a winner-take-all absolutism, jeopardizes the future. It is the royal, pragmatic "both/and" that reality requires, both Ahab and Ben-hadad, both Israel and Syria; but such pragmatic both/and is perceived by this prophet as both "Yahweh and Baal."

Such a theological compromise is not indicated at all in the narrative, but the radicality of "or" escalates and extrapolates, willing to sacrifice everything for some remembered or imagined purity.

Unlike my reading of the other prophetic narratives in this collection, and somewhat as a surprise, this narrative suggests to me an appreciation of the pragmatic "both/and" of the king. The narrative itself makes no comment on the matter. It is likely, in context, that the narrator is in sympathy with the prophetic verdict on Ahab and his realm. One cannot be sure, but it is probable. The stance of the prophet is, in the end, driven ideologically. The problem, of course, is that the line between faith and ideology is thin and elusive.[4] Stern, so it seems to me, is innocent of ideology and takes things too much at face value in his analysis. And where there is no critical awareness of the numbing power of ideology, the prophetic "or" becomes totally credible in the face of pragmatism.

One can, without any trouble, notice the absolute "or" as it besets the church (on such varied issues as sexuality, economics, and multiculturalism as it entangles whole societies, as in Northern Ireland or the Balkans), and even as it besets interpretive communities who pretend "objectivity" but in fact practice a "take no prisoners" acrimony. In my reading of it, this narrative invites a pause of appreciation for the "either" of royal practicality in the face of the uncritical prophetic "or." Finally, we must look in the wisdom of Israel for a "both/and" that resists an excessively innocent "or":

> He put before them another parable: "The kingdom of heaven may be compared to someone who sowed good seed in his field; but while everybody was asleep, an enemy came and sowed weeds among the wheat, and then went away. So when the plants came up and bore grain, then the weeds appeared as well. And the slaves of the householder came and said to him, 'Master, did you not sow good seed in our field? Where, then, did these weeds come from?' He answered, 'An enemy has done this.' The slaves said to him, 'Then do you want us to go and gather them?' But he replied, 'No; for in gathering the weeds you would uproot the wheat along with them. Let both of them grow together until the harvest; and at harvest time I will tell the reapers, 'Collect the weeds first and bind them in bundles to be burned, but gather the wheat into my barn.'" (Mt. 13:24–30)

The "or"—on economics, on sexuality, on politics, on interpretive method—often seems clear enough. It is not, however, always as near to harvest time as the advocates of "or" seem to imagine. It could be that an "or" too vigorous is an attempt to seize the initiative and preempt the harvest before its time. While such a zealous act of seizure may seem to its agents like faith, it is possible that such a seizure is a preemptive act that violates the one who said, "I am Yahweh." Thus, as the sage has observed, there is,

> a time to kill, and a time to heal;
> a time to love, and a time to hate;
> a time for war, and a time for peace (Eccl. 3:3, 8).

Ahab judged it was a time to heal, to love, to make peace. These prophetic figures think not; they imagine they always know what time it is, always the same time, always a time to kill, always a time to hate, always a time for war. In the real world Ahab has to be more tentative. Perhaps so should we, at least sometimes.

Conclusion

The prophetic narratives are not contemporaneous to us and need not be made contemporaneous. They are not relevant to our lives, and no effort is made here to make them relevant. Indeed, making the Bible "relevant" is a most hazardous enterprise, sure to be laden with ideological tilt. It belongs to such narratives, rather, that the stories can be retold and reheard more or less on their own terms, because they will have their own say, our preferences notwithstanding. Thus, we may take these stories as very old testimony to an alternative social reality that has at its core this irascible, generative character, Yahweh. The narratives make no concession to our modern or postmodern environment, but let us listen and then go from there as we are able.

I suggest, moreover, that it was ever so with these stories. I imagine that the very first tellers and listeners to these stories were completely nonplused by them. They did not know what to make of them; they could not, however, relinquish them and did not forget them, because they recognized that there was more yet to be given in their retelling and rehearing. In the later generations of the exile—perhaps the canonizing generations—they would not relinquish these tales, even though the stories were remote from lived reality and even though the stories would not give much concrete guidance or resource for coping with Babylon or Persia or, later, the forces of Hellenization. And yet they were told and heard yet again.

These stories, of course, arise in "a world behind the text" to which we have very little access. But clearly, these stories from early on are not acts of nostalgic remembering but are offers of "worlds in front of the text" that both summon and reassure. The books of Kings would be dreary indeed without these narratives and the characters embedded in them. The loss of such voicings of summons and reassurance would, moreover, have depleted the exilic generations that canonized them. In every generation of listeners, these narratives have invited imaginative alternative and have provided the materials for such conviction. This testimony is the offer of an uncensored, unfettered articulation of One beyond the ordinary who is enacted through human agency; hearing imaginatively is the responding act that takes this testimony, grounded so old and deep, and connects it to present life in a way never before conjured, that is, never before the new hearing.

Thus, the interconnection of testimony (as unfettered truth-telling of a concrete kind always awaiting adjudication) with imagination (as the capacity to host a world other than the one self-evident) is the generative moment of linkage between ancient text and contemporary contexts for faith. The testimony of these ancient narratives, already deeply permeated at the outset by imagination, makes available materials for the demanding work of faith in a society that is now largely defined by the global economy with its mesmerizing technologies and its disorienting pluralism. In that context, there is a great temptation to imagine that deep choices are no longer available and that the present global system, power, and money have closed off all alternatives. In that environment, the practice of faith entails courageous imagination, grounded by trusted texts that may yield otherwise. The narratives (and their key characters) endlessly insist that there are choices to be made (either/or) that hold the option of otherwise. These narratives (and others like them so deeply grounded with the same characters) may be the key resource for communities of faith to continue to live and breathe and sing and pray and act freely in an indifferent or hostile cultural environment.

I propose that such funding of the capacity for otherwise was the function of these narratives, in their initial tellings, in their exilic retellings, and in their endless later context-specific retellings. Royal time lines, military hardware, and domesticated religion have always surrounded these stories as they do in the books of Kings, hoping to lure listeners into despair. All of these accouterments of settled society do not, however, have the authority to silence the telling and the retelling, to curb the listening and the relistening. Such attestations as these stories voice, at their most daring and subversive, simply refuse to be submitted to universal reason or positivistic history. Perhaps a small but decisive indication of this refusal and its complementary resilience is the final notice in 2 Kings 13:20–21 that even the dead bones of Elisha gave life to a dead man. The exclamation that "he still gives life" is not unlike the reported last word of Galileo, "But it does move!" That notice in 2 Kings 13 asserts that this haunting human agency of life still lives in death and still gives life in the grave, still does "great things" beyond every expectation. Those who hear such attestation each time have to rethink and reimagine everything. The narratives bespeak such vitality, grounded in holiness, that all of the shutdowns of death are seen to be impotent in the face of daring retellings and attentive rehearings.

Notes

Introduction

[1]Walter Brueggemann, *Theology of the Old Testament: Testimony, Dispute, Advocacy* (Minneapolis: Fortress Press, 1997), 117–44 and passim.

[2]For a useful critique of my categories, see Norman K. Gottwald, "Rhetorical, Historical, and Ontological Counterpoints in Doing Old Testament Theology," *God in the Fray: A Tribute to Walter Brueggemann,* ed. Tod Linafelt and Timothy K. Beal (Minneapolis: Fortress Press, 1998), 11–23.

[3]I take the phrase "Chain of Voices" from Andre Brink, *Chain of Voices* (London: Faber, 1982).

[4]See my general discussion in Walter Brueggemann, *1 & 2 Kings,* Smyth & Helwys Bible Commentary (Macon: Smith & Helwys, 2000).

[5]For one attempt at canonical reflection on the books of Kings, see Brevard S. Childs, *Introduction to the Old Testament as Scripture* (Philadelphia: Fortress Press, 1979), 287–301. In his conclusion, Childs comments (300–301):"A canonical approach would see the intention of the biblical writer to describe the execution of the curses of Deuteronomy, which had been rehearsed by successive generations of prophets, against a disobedient covenant people." This comment would seem especially to connect the final form of the text to the crisis of exile, but Childs in the end would presumably eschew any such historical connection.

Chapter 1: An Imaginative "Or"

[1]Jon D. Levenson, *The Death and Resurrection of the Beloved Son: The Transformation of Child Sacrifice in Judaism and Christianity* (New Haven: Yale University Press, 1993) has explored Jewish antecedents to the Christian foundation of "Father-Son."

[2]For a critical summary of Newbigin's accent on ecclesiology, see George R. Hunsberger, *Bearing the Witness of the Spirit: Lesslie Newbigin's Theology of Cultural Pluralism* (Grand Rapids: Eerdmans, 1998).

[3]See Walter Brueggemann, "Ecumenism as the Shared Practice of a Peculiar Identity," *Word & World* 18 (Spring, 1998) 122–35.

[4]See my discussion, Walter Brueggemann, *Cadences of Home: Preaching Among Exiles* (Louisville: Westminster John Knox Press, 1997).

[5]The either/or I will exposit is essentially that of the Deuteronomic theology that speaks with conviction that one choice is good and one is bad (see Deut. 30:15–20). That is to say that the *either/or* of the Deuteronomist is completely without the irony of which Søren Kierkegaard (*Either/Or I,* trans. Howard V. Hong and Edna H. Hong [Princeton: Princeton University Press, 1987], 38–39), writes:

"Marry, and you will regret it. Do not marry, and you will also regret it. Marry or do not marry, you will regret it either way. Whether you marry or you do not marry, you will regret it either way. Laugh at the stupidities of the world, and you will regret it; weep over them, and you will also regret it. Laugh at the stupidities of

131

the world or weep over them, you will regret it either way. Whether you laugh at the stupidities of the world or you weep over them, you will regret it either way. Trust a girl, and you will regret it. Do not trust her, and you will also regret it. Trust a girl or do not trust her, you will regret it either way. Whether you trust a girl or do not trust her, you will regret it either way. Hang yourself, and you will regret it. Do not hang yourself, and you will also regret it. Hang yourself or do not hang yourself, you will regret it either way. Whether you hang yourself or do not hang yourself, you will regret it either way. This, gentlemen, is the quintessence of all the wisdom of life."

[6]It is instructive that in both narratives of Abraham (Gen. 15:6) and Moses (Ex. 4:1), the key term is *'amen* = "trust." It is "trust" that makes the "or" of Yahweh choosable against the "either" that characteristically seems given and easy to embrace.

[7]Of that intentional decision, Jacob Neusner, *The Enchantments of Judaism: Rites of Transformation from Birth Through Death* (New York: Basic Books, 1987), 212, writes, "All of us are Jews through the power of our imagination."

[8]Gerhard von Rad, *The Problem of the Hexateuch and Other Essays* (New York: McGraw-Hill, 1966), 73–74, 96, to be sure, takes chapter 24 to be an early credo and Josh. 21:43–45 to be the culmination of the Hexateuch. The placement of chapter 24, however, is important to the argument concerning its significance, even if he regards it as early.

[9]See Walter Brueggemann, *Biblical Perspectives on Evangelism: Living in a Three-Storied Universe* (Nashville: Abingdon Press, 1993), 48–70.

[10]Von Rad, *The Problem of the Hexateuch*, 6–7.

[11]On narratives producing worlds, see Amos Wilder, "Story and Story-World," *Interpretation* 37 (1983), 353–64.

[12]The term "far be it from" is an exceedingly strong expression, suggesting the complete inappropriateness of the action, for such an action would profane and render its subject unworthy. See a usage with reference to Yahweh's own action in Gen. 18:25.

[13]On this negative command, see the parallel in Gen. 35:1–4. Some scholars, following Albrecht Alt, suggest that a ritual performance is here envisioned whereby the foreign gods are dramatically banished from the community.

[14]The fundamental rhetorical analysis is that of Claus Westermann, "Sprache und Struktur der Prophetie Deuterojesajas," *Neudrucke und Berichte aus dem 20.Jahrhundert,* ThB 24 Altes Testament (München: Kaiser Verlag, 1964), 92–170.

[15]See Walter Brueggemann, *Theology of the Old Testament: Testimony, Dispute, Advocacy* (Minneapolis: Fortress Press, 1997), 117–44.

[16]It is evident that "testimony" is a way to make a claim from "below," when one lacks the tools and authority to make a more established sort of claim for truth. See my comments on Ricoeur and Wiesel, ibid.

[17]See Walter Brueggemann, *Biblical Perspectives on Evangelism*, especially 26–30.

[18]The most fundamental analysis is that of Jacques Ellul, *Technological Society* (New York: Random House, 1967). See more specifically to our point, Jacques Ellul, *The Humiliation of the Word* (Grand Rapids: Eerdmans, 1985).

[19]On the integrity of speech and matching speech to life, see Wendell Berry, *Standing by Words: Essays* (San Francisco: North Point Press, 1983), 24–63. A measure of the gravity of utterance for the truth of Yahweh is indicated in the often-cited Midrash on Isa. 43:10: "You are my witnesses, says the LORD." The Rabbis interpreted this as meaning: "If you are my witnesses, I am God, but if you are not my witnesses, I am not God." See Michael Oppenheim, *Speaking/Writing God: Jewish Philosophical Reflections on the Life with Others* (Albany: SUNY Press, 1997), 163. To this quote

Oppenheim adds: "And now it must be added: without Her witnesses, both God and we are lost."

[20]In recent time, Paul Ricoeur has understood most clearly and most consistently that serious religious language must be spoken in "figure," thus his accent on imagination. Speech that is not in "figure" runs the prompt risk of idolatry, of producing what can be controlled. See the several essays in his book nicely entitled *Figuring the Sacred: Religion, Narrative, and Imagination*, ed. Mark I. Wallace (Minneapolis: Fortress Press, 1995).

[21]See a summary of this scholarship by Terence E. Fretheim, *Deuteronomic History*, Interpreting Biblical Texts (Nashville: Abingdon Press, 1983).

[22]On this pivotal command, see Jeffries M. Hamilton, *Social Justice and Deuteronomy: The Case of Deuteronomy 15*, SBL Dissertation Series 136 (Atlanta: Scholars Press, 1992).

[23]See Walter Brueggemann, "Faith with a Price," *The Other Side* 34/4 (July & August, 1998), 32–35.

[24]The "or" of covenantal power is nicely put in the words of Jesus in Mk. 10:42–44.

[25]On neighborliness extended to outsiders and the weak insiders, see Lk. 4:26–27.

[26]See Grace I. Emmerson, *Isaiah 56—66*, Old Testament Guides (Sheffield: Sheffield Academic Press, 1992), and Elizabeth Achtemeier, *The Community and Message of Isaiah 56—66* (Minneapolis: Augsburg, 1982).

[27]The New Testament counterpart to such "foreigners and eunuchs" is perhaps "publicans and sinners," on which see Mk. 2:15–17.

[28]On neighborly attentiveness as a condition of well-being, see Mt. 25:31–46.

[29]Among the most helpful treatments of the parables is John R. Donahue, *The Gospel in Parable: Metaphor, Narrative, and Theology in the Synoptic Gospels* (Philadelphia: Fortress Press, 1988).

[30]Gerhard von Rad, *Wisdom in Israel* (Nashville: Abingdon Press, 1972), 65.

Chapter 2: The Faithfulness of "Otherwise"

[1]Paul Ricoeur, of course, is the dominant source for the current discussion of imagination. See, for example, "The Bible and the Imagination," *Figuring the Sacred: Religion, Narrative, and Imagination*, ed. Mark I. Wallace (Minneapolis: Fortress Press, 1995), 144–66. Surely as important is the use of imagination by Karl Barth, on which see Timothy Gorringe, *Karl Barth: Against Hegemony* (Oxford: Oxford University Press, 1999), 268–90, especially the references on pp. 283–86.

[2]By the use of the term "otherwise," I intend to allude to Emmanuel Levinas, *Otherwise than Being or Beyond Essence* (Boston: Martinus Nijhoff Publishers, 1981).

[3]On "the myth of the given," see especially Mary B. Hesse in a variety of publications. See, for example, "Criteria of Truth in Science and Theology," represented as "Concepts of Creation and Scientific Understanding," *Religious Studies* 11 (1975) 385–400; "Cosmology as Myth," *Cosmology and Theology*, ed. David Tracy and Nicholas Lash, Concilium 166 (San Francisco: Harper, 1983), 49–54; "Physics, Philosophy, and Myth," *Physics, Philosophy, and Theology*, ed. Robert J. Russell et. al. (Notre Dame: University of Notre Dame Press, 1988), 185–202; "Religion, Science, and Symbolism," *Religious Pluralism and Unbelief: Studies Critical and Comparative*, ed. Ian Hammett (London: Routledge, 1990), 166–78; "Science and Objectivity," *Habermas: Critical Debates*, ed. John B. Thompson and David Held (Cambridge, Mass.: MIT Press, 1982), 98–115.

[4]See Klaus Scholder, *The Birth of Modern Critical Theology: Origins and Problems of Biblical Criticism in the Seventeenth Century* (Philadelphia: Trinity Press International, 1990).

[5]For this material, most helpful to me have been Paul Hazard, *The European Mind: The Critical Years 1680–1715* (New York: Fordham University Press, 1990), and Stephen Toulmin, *Cosmopolis: The Hidden Agenda of Modernity* (New York: The Free Press, 1990). See my summary statement, Walter Brueggemann, *Texts Under Negotiation: The Bible and Post Modern Imagination* (Minneapolis: Fortress Press, 1993), chap. 1.

[6]See Richard Kearney, *The Wake of Imagination: Toward a Postmodern Culture* (Minneapolis: University of Minnesota Press, 1988).

[7]Walter Isaacson and Thomas Evan, *The Wise Men: Six Friends and the World They Made* (New York: Simon and Schuster, 1986).

[8]Robert S. McNamara and Brian Vandermark, *In Retrospect: The Tragedy & Lessons of Vietnam* (New York: Random House, 1995).

[9]Francis Fukuyama, *The End of History & the Last Man* (New York: Free Press, 1992). In a subsequent book, *Trust: The Social Virtues and the Creation of Prosperity* (New York: The Free Press, 1995), Fukuyama has perhaps sought to modify his claim slightly, but not much.

[10]On evangelical subversion of givenness, see Timothy Gorringe, *Karl Barth: Against Hegemony* (New York: Oxford University Press, 1999). Gorringe's discussion concerns Barth's stance regarding political hegemony. He does not extend the question to include intellectual or theological or economic or moral hegemony, though the point is deeply implicit in Barth's perspective. It does happen that the "Barthian tradition" itself is on occasion tempted to its own version of hegemonic domination.

[11]Michael Polanyi, *Personal Knowledge: Towards a Post-Critical Philosophy* (Chicago: University of Chicago Press, 1958).

For an acute theological reflection on the work of Polanyi, see Lesslie Newbigin, *Proper Confidence: Faith, Doubt & Certainty in Christian Discipleship* (Grand Rapids: Eerdmans, 1995).

[12]On the split of "fact" and "value," see Lesslie Newbigin, *Foolishness to the Greeks: The Gospel and Western Culture* (Grand Rapids: Eerdmans, 1986).

[13]Thomas Kuhn, *The Structure of Scientific Revolutions* (Chicago: University of Chicago Press, 1962).

[14]Alasdair MacIntyre, *Three Rival Versions of Moral Enquiry: Encyclopedia, Genealogy, and Tradition* (Notre Dame: University of Notre Dame Press, 1990); and *Whose Justice? Which Rationality?* (Notre Dame: University of Notre Dame Press, 1989).

[15]Charles Taylor, *Sources of the Self: The Making of the Modern Identity* (Cambridge: Cambridge University Press, 1989).

[16]On the "masters of suspicion," see Paul Ricoeur, *Freud and Philosophy: An Essay on Interpretation* (New Haven: Yale University Press, 1970). The work of Derrida, Foucault, and Levinas in quite different ways are congruent with Ricoeur's program of suspicion.

[17]See Geoffrey H. Hartman and Sanford Budick, eds., *Midrash and Literature* (New Haven: Yale University Press, 1986); and Susan A. Handelman, *The Slayers of Moses: The Emergence of Rabbinic Interpretation in Modern Literary Theory* (Albany: SUNY Press, 1983).

[18]With specific reference to the parables as "limit expressions," see Paul Ricoeur, "Biblical Hermeneutics," *Semeia* 4 (1975), 107–45.

[19]On the relation of *say* and *get*, see Walter Brueggemann, *Theology of the Old Testament: Testimony, Dispute, Advocacy* (Minneapolis: Fortress Press, 1997), 117–44. It is impossible to overestimate the decisive importance of the exact articulation of Israel for the God who is "given and gotten" in the text of the Old Testament.

[20]John D. O'Banion, *Reorienting Rhetoric: The Dialectic of List and Story* (University Park, Pa.: Pennsylvania State University Press, 1992).

[21]Ibid., 108.

[22]Along with Elijah and Elisha, attention should be paid to Micaiah ben Imlah (1 Kings 22), perhaps the most generative of any of these prophetic narratives. I have, however, limited my attention to Elijah for practical reasons.

[23]On the history of critical scholarship—with particular reference to Hermann Gunkel—and its residue of problems, see Rick D. Moore, *God Saves! Lessons from the Elisha Stories*, JSOT Supp. 95 (Sheffield: JSOT Press, 1990).

[24]While "as if" seems a correct rendering of the way the parables are presented, I might prefer simply "as" that concedes nothing about "reality." On the "copula of imagination," see Garrett Green, *Imagining God: Theology & the Religious Imagination* (San Francisco: Harper and Row, 1989), 73 and passim..

[25]J. R. R. Tolkien, "Tree and Leaf," *The Tolkien Reader* (New York: Ballantine Books, 1966), 68–75 and passim offers a nice distinction between fantasy and imagination.

[26]Above all, it has been Richard Kearney who has insisted upon and explored the ways in which imagination is an ethical undertaking. See *Wake of Imagination* (St. Paul: University of Minnesota Press, 1987), *Poetics of Imagining* (London: Routledge, 1991), and *Poetics of Modernity: Toward a Hermeneutic Imagination* (Atlantic Highlands: Humanities Press, 1995). In the latter, see his discussions of Levinas, Derrida, and especially Jan Patocka.

[27]So careful a critical exegete as Bernhard Anderson has seen that imagination permits freedom under the discipline of the text, and is not indiscriminate fantasy. Anderson, *Contours of Old Testament Theology* (Minneapolis: Fortress Press, 1999), 36, writes:

"But the symbolic power of the language transcends the social location and the historical circumstances in which it was originally expressed and was released with new power when the tradition became *scripture* for the community of faith. The task of the biblical theologian is to enter and understand the biblical world(s) construed by imagination. When the symbolism finds an echo in our poetic response, as 'deep calls to deep' (cf. Ps. 42:7), the Bible may speak today with the power of the word of God."

[28]Richard B. Hays, *The Moral Vision of the New Testament: Community, Cross, New Creation—A Contemporary Introduction to New Testament Ethics* (San Francisco: Harper, 1996), 298–99.

[29]For a powerful model of such imaginative construal, see Ellen F. Davis, *Imagination Shaped: Old Testament Preaching in the Anglican Tradition* (Valley Forge: Trinity Press International, 1995).

Chapter 3: Miracle and Accommodation

[1]The sign of the critical judgment that narrative is less than convincing about "history" is the term "legend," given its dominant force in Old Testament studies by Hermann Gunkel, "Introduction: The Legends of Genesis," *Genesis,* trans. Mark E. Biddle (Macon: Mercer University Press, 1997), vii–lxix. Gunkel, ix, writes:

"The most obvious characteristic of legend is that it frequently reports extraordinary things incredible to us. The reality of this poetry differs from the reality pertinent to prosaic life and ancient Israel also considered many things possible that seem impossible to us. Thus, Genesis reports many things that contradict our advanced knowledge."See also Jay A. Wilcoxen, "Narrative," *Old Testament Form Criticism,* ed. John H. Hayes (San Antonio: Trinity University Press, 1974), 58–98.

[2]On the "myth of the given," see Wilfrid Sellars, *Science, Perception & Reality* (Atascadero, Calif.: Ridgeview, 1991), as well as the work of Mary Hesse.

[3]The urgency and irony of the narrative will be missed unless the reader recognizes the depth of dread connected to the term "leprosy." While the disease may be physically costly, the deeper cost is social isolation and exclusion, surely not unlike the current "dread" over AIDS. In addition to the Priestly attention to the social disease of leprosy (Leviticus 13—14), see the theological verdict on Uzziah in 2 Chr. 26:16–23. In commenting on the healing of the leper in Mark 1:40–45, Fernando Belo, *A Materialist Reading of the Gospel of Mark* (Maryknoll: Orbis Books, 1981), 106, comments that the act of healing was "the subversion of this symbolic order." In our narrative the prophet Elisha does nothing less than to subvert an entire symbolic ordering of society. It is this social reality that gives thickness to the narrative.

[4]The Torah of Israel entertains the legitimate possibility of the seizure and retention of a "beautiful woman" taken by the Israelites as a captive of war; thus, the Syrian act was surely not different from that of the horizon of Israel. See Deut. 21:10–14, though perhaps verse 14 is a light restraint on the primal freedom of male members of the community. On the patriarchal construction of social relationships reflected in such law see Harold C. Washington, "Violence and the Construction of Gender in the Hebrew Bible: A New Historicist Approach," *Biblical Interpretation* 5/4 (1997), 324–63, and Carolyn Pressler, *The View of Women Found in the Deuteronomic Family Laws,* BZAW 216 (Berlin: De Gruyter, 1993).

[5]The specificity of the Syrian god Rimmon is not particularly important for the narrative, except that this is a god other than the God of Israel. Rimmon is known elsewhere to be the Syrian equivalent to Baal. There may be some irony in this latter point, as the prophetic narratives concerning Elijah and Elisha, during the dynasty of Omri, are deeply opposed to Baal. It may be that this narrative is not concerned that Rimmon may be Baal in another form, or that this narrative in particular is not interested in the characteristic polemic made against Baalism during the Omri dynasty. Either way, Elisha's response to the anticipation of the Syrian general upon his return home is quite remarkable.

[6]The request for pardon on the lips of the Syrian is most remarkable, perhaps not unlike the petition of Pharaoh in Exodus 9:27, 10:16–17, though with different terminology. On the general capacity and occasional refusal of YHWH to forgive, see Walter Brueggemann, "The Travail of Pardon: Reflections on *slh,*" (forthcoming).

[7]The response of Elisha to the general, "Go in peace," is unexpected, given the usual polemic in these narratives against gods rival to YHWH. The response may indicate, narratively presented, that Elisha in this episode has broken from that usual life-or-death polemic. In any case, the response provides a resource for thinking again about pluralism in contemporary discussion.

[8]While there are physical, medical dimensions to leprosy, it is clear that the narrative thinks primarily in theological categories. As the healing of leprosy is a blessing, so the assignation of leprosy is surely understood theologically as a curse. Elisha is of course completely capable of both actions commensurate with YHWH, a God of blessing and curse.

Chapter 4: The Good News of Bread

[1]I am unable to locate a citation for the phrase with which Niles is famously connected. His granddaughter has told me that very likely the phrase was originally from Willem Visser t'Hooft, though Niles appropriated it and gave it broad currency.

[2]Larry L. Lyke, *King David with the Wise Woman of Tekoa: The Resonance of Tradition in Parabolic Narrative,* JSOT Supp. 255 (Sheffield: Sheffield Academic Press, 1997), 104–7.

[3]There is some little confusion in the text in these verses. The intent, however, is clear, and I am following a conventional scholarly ordering of the text.

[4]The term "trouble" (*ra*) here is not the same term as in 1 Kings 18:17. The negative sentiment, however, is the same.

[5]See Walter Brueggemann, *Biblical Perspectives on Evangelism: Living in a Three-Storied Universe* (Nashville: Abingdon Press, 1993), 14–47.

[6]Ibid., 26–30 and passim.

Chapter 5: Tell Me All the Great Things

[1]David Jobling, *I Samuel* (New York: Liturgical Publications, 1998) has made clear that "the Philistines" function as the epitome of "the other" that is threat. The fact that the woman finds food among "the other" and not in Israel is a powerful piece of irony.

[2]On this litigious practice in the text, see Richard N. Boyce, *The Cry to God in the Old Testament,* SBL Dissertation Series 103 (Atlanta: Scholars Press, 1988).

[3]This vocabulary characteristically is matched to a variety of verbs, most often *za'aq, sa'aq, gara'*. See Psalms 9:12; 17:1; 22:5; 34:17; 77:1–2; 106:44; 107:6, 13, 19, 28; 119:169.

[4]Here I have mentioned only those terms used in the doxological catalogue of Ps. 145:4–7. Israel's rich vocabulary on this subject included other terms as well, such as *mophôth* and *pa'al*.

[5]On testimony as the utterance of new reality, see Brueggemann, *Theology of the Old Testament: Testimony, Advocacy, Dispute* (Minneapolis: Fortress Press, 1997), 117–44 and passim.

[6]On the power of testimony to mediate "news" from there to here, from then to now, see Walter Brueggemann, *Biblical Perspectives on Evangelism: Living in a Three-Storied Universe* (Nashville: Abingdon Press, 1993).

Chapter 6: The Overstated Prophetic "Or"

[1]Walther Zimmerli, *I Am Yahweh* (Atlanta: John Knox Press, 1982).

[2]To entertain a parallel of this military consultation to a recent encounter like "The Cuban Missile Crisis" is enormously illuminating. On the Kennedy record of that encounter, see Ernest R. May and Philip D. Zeliko, eds., *The Kennedy Tapes: Inside the White House During the Cuban Missile Crisis* (Cambridge, Mass.: Belknap Press, 1997).

[3]See Philip D. Stern, *The Biblical Herem: A Window on Israel's Religious Experience* (Atlanta: Scholars Press, 1991), 178–83.

[4]On the thin, delicate, crucial line between faith and ideology, see Patrick D. Miller, "Faith and Ideology in the Old Testament," *Magnalia Dei, The Mighty Acts of God: Essays on the Bible and Archaeology in Memory of G. Ernest Wright,* ed. Frank M. Cross et. al. (Garden City: Doubleday & Co., 1976), 464–79.

Scripture Index